Other books by R. Karl Largent:
Black Death
Ancients
Pagoda
The Prometheus Project
The Witch of Sixkill
The Lake
Red Tide
Red Ice
Red Skies
Red Sand
Red Wind
The Sea
Getting Started... Handbook for the Beginning Novelist
The Job Game... Preparing to Win... Workbook for Resume Writers
Write Tight and Right... Workbook for Business Writers

as Robin Karl:
Amityville – The Nightmare Continues

as Simon Lawrence:
The Pond

How do I get published?

This book is for every writer who has asked the question, 'How do I get published?' It may be that you have a dusty manuscript in a closet or this could be your first venture into writing for publication; either way you will find tips, tricks, and helpful advice within these pages from professional writers who at some point in their lives asked the very same question.

EDITOR'S NOTE

There are, as usual, far too many people to thank in the space I have here, so to those omitted I offer my sincere regrets. I must, however, cite some of those people without whose assistance this book would not exist: Geneva S. Blaising's skills were invaluable in laying out the book, Stephanie Keenan who supplied helpful advice, Mark Ruebling, our favorite reader, who always gives us a different perspective, Dr. Earl Conn for his foreword and other valuable assistance, Terri Willits for her typesetting ability, and of course, the wonderful writers who supplied us with a great deal of information on how they practice their craft.

I would like to personally thank the author, R. Karl Largent, for bringing this project to me. We've had some wonderful adventures together, my friend. May we look back on this one fondly.

And finally, on behalf of Karl and myself, thank you to our wives, Wilma and Pam, who have shown us more love, support, and understanding than we probably deserve. This one's for you, kids. Thanks. We love you.

Matthew V. Clemens
Davenport, Iowa

Contents

ASSASSINATION, FOUR WORDS, CUSSLER, AND
A WRITERS CONFERENCE..xiii

GETTING PUBLISHED – WHAT'S IT ALL ABOUT............xvi

HUMOR
Kathryn Hammer..18

HOW I WRITE A ROMANCE
Lauren M. Phelps...30

THE ROMANCE MARKET – AN OVERVIEW
M. Sue Lemmon...35

CREATING YOUR OWN FOUNTAIN OF YOUTH
David R. Collins...38

THE CHILDREN'S BOOK MARKET – AN OVERVIEW
Mel Boring..42

HOW TO WRITE THE ONLY TRUE AMERICAN GENRE
Wendi Lee..48

AN OVERVIEW OF THE MARKET FOR WESTERNS
Vince Matthews...53

THE MYSTERY OF WRITING MYSTERIES
Max Allan Collins..54

HOW TO WRITE TRUE CRIME
Pat Gipple & Matthew V. Clemens..58

TRUE CRIME MARKET – AN OVERVIEW
Matthew V. Clemens...63

HOW I WRITE TECHNO-THRILLERS
R. Karl Largent..64

THE POET'S VIEW
Glenna Glee...70

WHAT I LOOK FOR IN A GOOD (WEEKLY) NEWSPAPER ARTICLE or HINTS FROM THE EDITOR FROM HELL
Viv Sade-Rosswurm...74

IF YOU WANT TO WRITE ABOUT ENTERTAINMENT... READ THIS (AND THEN DECIDE)
Linda Cook...86

SELF-PUBLISHING
Jana Lynn Shellman..94

THE BOOK DOCTOR: WHY I GET PAID TO DO WHAT I DO
Matthew V. Clemens..106

REASSEMBLING THE DUST
Wes. D. Gehring...110

THE SUBMISSION PACKAGE..116

AGENTS..146

MAKING A LIVING AS A WRITER
Alan Garinger...154

... MORE THOUGHTS ON HOW TO MAKE A BUCK OR TWO BY WRITING
R. Karl Largent..164

THE PROS OF HOW THE PROS DO IT..............................170

FOREWORD

What a great idea!

Karl Largent – no stranger to good ideas – certainly has come up with one here.

Gathered together in this volume is the best advice from the best writers about getting published. First, he has asked nearly 20 writers to share what they have learned throughout their careers in writing and publishing. You would have to attend lots of workshops and conduct lots of interviews to get the equivalent of all this information. Then, he shows you how to market your work with specific examples of everything you might need.

So, it's all here in one book. The writing is straightforward and no-nonsense. The advice is sound. The last section has been prepared by Karl himself, who has been enormously successful in these recent years since a colleague challenged him to set his excuses aside and get on with his writing. The last I knew, Karl was sending off to his publisher his 15th novel and gearing up for his 16th. In other words, the advice from Karl and others in this book is from the very people who have been there, done that.

I know there are a multitude of books around about the craft of writing. Many of them are excellent. All of us could benefit from reading or rereading them and applying their counsel to get off the mark, to retool, to explore more options, to improve our writing, to learn more about markets, to improve our own marketing.

Getting Published now joins a select list of the most helpful and best.

Earl L. Conn, Dean Emeritus
College of Communication, Information, and Media
Ball State University
Muncie, Indiana

Co-Director
Midwest Writers Workshop
Muncie, Indiana

INSPIRATION

ASSASSINATION, FOUR WORDS, CUSSLER, AND A WRITERS CONFERENCE

Looking back, I've told this story at almost every writer's seminar I've ever conducted, primarily because there is a moral to it. It is about writing (what else) and illustrates many of the precepts you are going to read as you work your way through this book. Oddly enough, it all starts with the assassination of President John F. Kennedy clear back in 1963.

Like so many of us, I sat glued to my television set during the three days that followed that dark hour in our history. The images, emotions, and sounds all left impressions that even today bring tears to my eyes when I see the videotapes of that sobering event.

A side effect of that event, however, changed my life. That side effect stems from the word "assassination." The assassination of a world leader, up until that time in my life, was a horrendous event that happened only in other "less civilized" countries. It certainly was not something that I had experienced, and it was not a subject to which I had given much thought. But there it was, our President was dead, and the course of our future had been altered.

The following spring, I took an excursion through the western half of the United States with my two sons. Our journeys eventually took us to Salt Lake City where I was fascinated by the information I discovered about Brigham Young. Here was a man who was a true visionary. The streets of Salt Lake City had been laid out, well over a hundred years ago, in such a fashion that they would accommodate even today's staggering traffic problems. Communications in the land he called Zion were far ahead of their

Getting Published

time, and he foresaw many of the social problems that still plague us. In short, Brigham Young was ahead of his time.

Returning from that trip, a curious thought occurred to me. What if Brigham Young had been assassinated before he had the opportunity to implement his visions? How would that have altered history in what we call the American West?

That thought wouldn't go away, and as naïve as it sounds today, I decided to write a fictionalized version of an attempt to assassinate Brigham Young. After what I considered adequate research efforts, I sat down and churned out a 360 page novel about an insurrection within the Church of Latter Day Saints and a failed attempt to assassinate its leader.

Had I ever written anything before? No. Did I know what I was doing? No. I sent the book off to an agent in New York, and six weeks later, miracle of miracles (though I didn't know it was a miracle at the time) I received a comprehensive seven page letter that outlined the changes that needed to be made in order to make the novel saleable.

Lots of changes? Yeah. But you know what I thought? I thought the letter meant the agent didn't like my work. So I put the book away and didn't make another attempt to write fiction for almost twenty years.

Let's fast forward now to the early 80s and a business trip to California. I had completed my assignment and was preparing to return to our corporate headquarters in Columbus, Indiana. As I was boarding the plane and being congratulated by my peers for sewing up the deal, one of my colleagues asked me what was next on my agenda.

"Well," I said, "I still want to write a novel."

"What's holding you back?" he asked.

I paraded out all the standard excuses: no time, too busy, no place to write, and so on.

That's when my colleague cut me off with, looking back, probably the four most important words anyone has ever said to me,

INSPIRATION

"You could get started."

That must have been what educators like to call a "teachable moment," because that was when the message finally got through.

I started.

Then the third important thing happened. I went to a writer's conference. Specifically, the Midwest Writers Workshop at Ball State University in Muncie, Indiana. By that time I had churned out a couple of attempts at writing a novel, neither of which was worth showing to anyone. I was a little less naïve at that point and I knew that something was lacking, I just didn't know what. I knew I could tell a story, but I wasn't the writer I needed to be to get published.

Uncertain and hoping to find a way to climb to the next rung on the ladder of my writing career, I attended the conference. Once there, I began rubbing shoulders with, and learning from, real writers like Holly Miller, Alan Garinger, and Clive Cussler. When that conference ended, I was hooked. I had made that quantum leap into the world of commitment and discipline that it takes to become a writer.

One year later, I sold my first novel... and the idea for it actually crystallized on the drive home from that first writer's conference.

Getting Published

GETTING PUBLISHED – WHAT IT'S ALL ABOUT

"In the beginning... "

Isn't that a great way to begin a story? Is there a better way? Probably not. But even if there isn't, thousands upon thousands of writers, scribes, novelists, spinners of yarns, bards, and essayists have spent lifetimes searching for it.

Beginning a new book. Now that's exciting stuff.

That's what this is all about, the beginning – the beginning of your career as a writer. And the question for so many of us is, how can I get what I write (and here's that magic word) published?

Well, first things first. Before you have to worry about getting published, you have to have something to publish. Seems pretty obvious, doesn't it? But just in case the obvious has escaped some of us, here is one of the most fundamental rules of becoming published. In order to join the ranks of the published, you first must have written something that someone thinks is worth publishing.

All too apparent? Apparently not. Because one of the most frequently asked questions at my Mechanics of Writing a Novel seminar is, how can I get my works published?

"Do you have something ready to submit to a publishing house?" I ask.

The answer is usually, "No, but I've got this great idea and I want to know how I can get it published after I get it written."

Back to the obvious. If you don't have something ready to present to a publisher, and you are new to the writing game, your chances of getting your work published are slim indeed.

On the other hand, if you have written something and you are serious about submitting the work to a publisher, this is the book for you. This book is written for, by and about people who have been down the very road you seek to travel. For example: Max

INSPIRATION

Allan Collins, unprecedented six time nominee for the prestigious Shamus Award given to outstanding mystery writers, will discuss the intricacies of the commercial mystery novel. Wes Gehring, Professor of Film at Ball State University, and comedy historian, discusses the complexities of being a biographer for some of the greats and near greats of the cinematic world. And in her essay on self-publishing, Jana Lynn Shellman will tell you about the commitment and sacrifices she had to make to put her charming *The Wish Factory* on the market.

To be sure, there is more – a great deal more. Matthew Clemens and Pat Gipple, co-authors of the riveting *Dead Water*, will talk about the trials and tribulations of the true crime writer.

And that's not all. David R. Collins, noted children's author; Kathy Hammer, humor writer; Wendi Lee, author of westerns; and Lauren Phelps, romance writer, will tell you how they ply their trade as well. All of them are deservedly successful in their given fields.

But that's only part of the story. The second segment of *Getting Published* is a "how to" workshop.

In Part 2 of *Getting Published*, we will take you through the labyrinth of book proposals, showing you the correct way to package your submission regardless of whether you are selling fiction or non-fiction. You will also see an actual proposal that sold book-length works in the fiction and non-fiction categories.

You will find examples of cover letters, writers' resumes, and a synopsis. You will find a section on how to get an agent and how to survive without one.

Finally, Alan Garinger, educator and author, will discuss a wide variety of other ways to make money with your writing talents.

All of these elements will combine to give you inspiration, new ideas, and tips on researching, saving time, saving money, using a book doctor, as well as the road to travel toward *Getting Published*.

HUMOR
by Kathryn Hammer

I wish I had an exciting, glamorous story to share about the series of incredible coincidences and planetary convergencies that led to publication – ("*So*, despite the bullet wound to my head, I overpowered the hijackers, flew the crippled 747 to safety in the hurricane, and – can you believe it? – one of the oh-so-grateful passengers turned out to be a publishing magnate!")

A story like that would be so much more fun to tell than the real one. Plus, more people would believe me, because my story is excruciatingly pedestrian; a textbook case which, for its lack of drama, strikes people as, well, a little far-fetched. I wrote a manuscript, polished it, headed to the library and sat down with *Literary Market Place* and *Writers' Market*. I learned submission protocol, got names and addresses (which I called to confirm), wrote queries to agents and publishers and – waited.

See, I told you it was a crummy story. But, on the bright side, it is good news for a pre-published writer who, suspecting that book contracts are meted out in stingy portions only to the connected or convicted, despair of ever seeing their books in print. Take heart: *I had no inside track, no benevolent mentor, no basement full of bodies, nuthin.'* I didn't even have a sizzling topic or specialized expertise. What I did have was the same stuff available to you: a phone, a library, a bookstore, postage, a modicum of initiative and learning skills and a smidgen of chutzpah. I simply soaked everything I could from books just like this, then applied it. That's it. Really.

I tell my story at writers' conferences and, invariably, someone will challenge me. (Actually, "accuse" strikes a more accurate tone.) "You *had* to have some sort of edge!" The meaning is clear: I'm leaving something out, deliberately withholding The Ancient Druid Secret, and by God, they're gonna get it outta me.

It's an understandable reaction. Getting published **is** difficult. (If it weren't, it wouldn't be a big deal and we wouldn't want it so passionately, now, would we?) It's this difficulty, perhaps, that fosters

Getting Published

a dual climate of glamorous mystique and vague suspicions, a nigling certainty that getting published entails some sort of industry anointing or legacy or bestowal of The Ancient Secret by a member of The Official Publishing Tribunal. (Harboring this notion also insulates one's tender psyche from the pain of rejection. It's easier to accept that it's "the system," not our writing that's at issue.) As tempting and perversely consoling as this notion is, get it out of your head.

[Note: A permutation of this does, however, still linger in the back of my mind. While I do have confidence in my writing, I also know there are legions of talented writers out there who are not published. Knowing that I got into print by virtue of mere common sense and reading commonly available books and following directions (how dull), and knowing that it didn't take years and years of rejection slips and tortured anguish, I can't help but think, well, maybe this is all a mistake. Maybe I didn't suffer enough for it to be Official. I half expect that one of these days the Head Person in Charge of Reality is going to pull my file, call me up and say, 'I'm sorry, Ms. Hammer. There's been a terrible mistake. Get a job.']

Perhaps I feel this way because I'm having so much FUN; it just seems too good to be true – a feeling I wish on all of you! Because my road was not greased with "connections," I have a vaguely surreptitious feeling, like I've crashed an exclusive party, sneaking my way past the doorman without an invitation. All it took – and, if you're interested, this works for weddings and State Dinners as well – was to act like I belonged there.

Yup, that's pretty much it. Your query or proposal should indicate to the editor that you belong there. Of course, this means you have to know what the people who *do* belong there act like. "And how might *that* be?" you ask. I'm getting to that… but first, a pop quiz.

Why do publishers buy manuscripts? Because they are magnanimous patrons of the arts with unlimited capital and largesse whose only joy in life is providing exposure for talent? BZZZZZ. Wrong answer. Publishers do not reward good writers with book contracts. They INVEST in good writers. Grasp this and your book

HUMOR

is on its way to the bookshelf. Publishing is a business, which is why a businesslike approach is going to give you The Edge.

If I had to point to any "edge" I might have had, that would be it. I had a background in business and was not uncomfortable with the territory. So admittedly, it was somewhat easier for me to act like I knew what I was doing, because, to a degree, I did.

To tailor that knowledge, I lurked on on-line writers group discussions, familiarized myself with the queries and proposals of professional writers (available in scores of writers' books) and came up with my own version. I acted like a professional, and – surprise! – that's how I was treated. That was my "edge" – being businesslike.

"Businesslike?" you gasp, clutching at your throat, your eyes wide with terror. "I have to be *businesslike?*"

Dark clouds gather in the distance. "Are you not interested in The Ancient Druid Publishing Secret?" I intone ominously. (If this were a multi-media book, there would now be eerie organ music and maniacal laughter.)

"But," you wail, "I don't wanna know that stuff! Next thing, you'll be using the *s* word."

"Ah yes, the *s* word. *Sales.*" (More organ music. More maniacal laughter.)

You slap your hands over your ears. "I don't want to hear this. I'm a writer, fercryingoutloud, not a salesman! I shouldn't have to do this. My book will sell itself if only they'd read it!"

Uh-huh. And just how do you think you're going to get "them" to read it? By sending it off in a manila envelope? With thousands of books to chose from for your own reading, do you opt for one by unknown authors whose covers read only, 'Please oh puh-lease just give me a chance! I am really, really, REALLY good!"

You stick to favorite authors or books recommended by friends. Maybe you'll browse and select on the basis of the dust jacket. But you wouldn't dive into a pile of unmarked books and devour them cover to cover. And yet that's what an unsolicited manuscript in the slush pile is – which is why I'm writing with the presumption that you query. It's smart. It's businesslike.

Getting Published

Yes, I know there's a body of thought about humor submissions not being subject to the Query Laws of Nature. (Being "light," they float to the top of the slush pile or something, I dunno.) The logic is that humor is so subjective and personal it's incompatible with the standard query format; it can't convey the essence of your humor. It's a whole lot easier to just send off the whole wad. This may work with articles, but if my batting average with books counts for anything – three for three – I stand by the querying route. Because, even though the standards for humor manuscripts are different, you still have to get the sucker read. And it's just not a good bet that it will be lying there in the slush pile. Unless you've submitted to psychics, who knows it's a humor manuscript?

Okay, yes, stuff does get published over the transom. But the likelihood of it happening is abysmal. You're more apt to find Mel Gibson in your trunk. Write a query! It's your dust jacket.

If all this talk about business and sales kinda makes your skin crawl, you're not alone. A lot of writers, not just humorists, tend to scratch and scream and claw when advised to go down that path. It's far more comfortable to stay in creative mode. But professional writers realize that, like it or not, publishing is a business, and they act accordingly.

Businesses and industries each have their own particular conventions and protocols; flouting or ignoring them sends a signal that you're either out of your element or you're trouble. Publishing is no different. Yet too many writers disregard or alter the prescribed methods for queries and submissions. Allowing for the many who never bothered to find out what standard protocol was in the first place – which excludes you because you're reading this book – we are still left with an inexplicably large number of writers who know the drill, yet evidently choose not to follow it. Why?

My theory is they're smart. They're clever and they're thinking logically. It stands to reason that since every other pre-published writer follows the protocol, the by-the-book approach becomes so overused that any such submission gets lost in a sea of sameness. So they break the rule. If everyone is double spacing with the Courier 10, well then, by golly, *they're* gonna stand out by single spacing with Arial 20 font. And fluorescent fuschia paper oughta get some attention, dontcha think?

Makes sense. But this turns out to be one of those double-edged gotchas. The strategy backfires because – and this is from agents and editors and other published writers – a professional, businesslike query or proposal is NOT the norm; it's a rarity – a welcome, blessed deviation from that Unprofessional sea of sameness. Consequently, a well-written, businesslike query *will* get attention, for all the right reasons.

So my advice is slavish adherence to protocol. (It's the little details that trip up gatecrashers who don't belong at the party.) Ironically, conformity will make you stand out so your manuscript gets read.

Here's where, in a writers' conference, the hands shoot up with the "yeah-buts" and the "what-ifs." I know there are exceptions and, truly, I'm delighted at any successful crashing of the publishing party, no matter how it's done. But I can address myself only to my own observations, my own experience.

At first I was puzzled by resistance to seemingly simple advice until I recognized that, to some, my advice wasn't simple at all – it was downright scary. After developing and nurturing and honing their creative side and working their butts off wrenching manuscripts from their souls word by word, they are now being told that they must metamorphosize into businesspeople. Ack! Imagine if the roles were reversed – tell an accountant that oh, by the way, your job requires doing a little professional stand-up comedy – *whoa*! Apoplexy.

So it's likely a lack of business confidence that sends the pre-published humor writer in search of an escape hatch, a method compatible with the creative, unconventional self. But the necessary shift from creative mode to business mode need not be intimidating. Believe me when I say that if you have the capacity to write a saleable manuscript, you have the capacity to write a business letter, which is

Getting Published

all a query is. Truly, all the necessary info can be gleaned from existing books on submission protocol. (You don't actually have to *be* businesslike and professional – just act like you are. Remember, you're a creative person!) In addition to books aimed at writers, I suggest picking up a few generic business correspondence books; they'll give you a feel for tone, layout, and content.

"Ok, I'll buy that," you say. "But how can I be businesslike with humor? Shouldn't I be, um, *funny*?" Well, yes. You should be funny in the manuscript. But if you want it published, you have to get someone to read it first, which means a query.

But how on earth do you query humor? You can't just launch into a pitch like you would with straight non-fiction, stating the topic and itemizing the points. The topic is 90% immaterial because it's the author's style and execution that makes humor what it is. So your natural inclination is to try to showcase your style in the query – knock 'em dead with a dazzling display of your gut-busting wit, right?

Wrong.

Successful business people do not get cute in their business correspondence. And – post this on little sticky notes all over your computer – PUBLISHING *IS* A BUSINESS. So hold the cream pie and seltzer.

Romance writers don't attempt to entice editors with steamy, mushy queries detailing the carnal joys that await their milky white thighs if only they would read the manuscript. And what editor would request a police procedural manuscript from a writer whose proposal was dripping O-positive? Publishers follow the same basic rules of business observed by other for-profit organizations, i.e. it's just good practice to avoid contractual arrangements with lunatics.

Your job, remember, is to convince them that you're a potentially good investment. You do not convince them of this by begging, cajoling, pleading, threatening, insulting. Nor do you further your case by being cloyingly cute, sarcastic, hyperbolic, flip, or slapstick. Devices that may work in a humor manuscript fall flat in a query.

A query is, after all, the equivalent of an initial job interview at a – there's that word again – *business*. Would you show up in a personnel

HUMOR

office wearing clown shoes and Groucho glasses? Yes, you want to convince them that you're funny. But you first have to convince them that you're competent.

That's not to say your query should read like a stock offering prospectus. There's equal danger in going overboard with this seriousness schtick. Trust me, I know. My first batch of queries on my first book struck out royally. Having deduced that The Secret to crashing the publishing party was to be businesslike, I gave it to them in spades. Boy, was I professional! I also came across like a constipated governess, albeit a very professional one.

Rereading the query, I became painfully aware that the tone of the letter did not match the product. What in this letter, I asked myself, would make an editor think this stuffy, stilted woman could write funny? Nothing. Zip. Zero. Fortunately, I had only sent out a small handful. I rewrote.

The content remained largely unchanged but I altered the tone. A bit lighter, a bit breezier. I loosened my tie and let the editor see the twinkle in my eye, ending the query letter with a postscript: "Awaiting your response, I shall occupy my time eating Cool Whip directly from the tub. My thighs look forward to an early reply." I mailed them off. (The queries, not my thighs.)

How'd I fare? After dispatching six New & Improved Queries, within a week I had four positive responses to see the manuscript (two from agents, two from publishers). One editor's request for my manuscript included a hand-written tutorial on the proper way to eat Cool Whip – as a dip for Oreos. I sent off the book to all who asked, packing one manuscript box with – you guessed it! – Oreo cookies. A week later, I had an agent and a publisher.

I had crashed the party!

See why I'm harping on the query? An as-yet unread manuscript is prejudged by the query letter's content and demeanor. It's your first impression, your job interview. Remember, you want to look like you belong there! I knew enough not to show up at the job interview wearing a fright wig, Groucho glasses, and a squirting

Getting Published

corsage. But with the first query, I arrived in a tweed suit and orthopedic shoes when the job called for a red silk skirt. I most certainly did not look like I belonged.

With the second query, I hit the right mix of professionalism and comfortable lightheartedness. Ironically, compliance with the conventions of business gave me license to be a bit silly in the postscript. Had I been a frenetic Jerry Lewis throughout, I could not have gotten away with it. Even my stationery conveys a sense of professionalism; I've been told it looks like an attorney's letterhead. (Maybe that's because I deliberately chose paper and typeface used by lawyers. Funny how that works. Funny how my letters all get opened.)

I can now hear you saying, yeah, right, sending Oreos sounds *real* professional.

Ah yes, but timing comes into play. After having established in the query an impression of being businesslike, I then – and only then – had the latitude to get a little creative with the cookies. The editor gave the signal; I responded. Had I sent Cool Whip or Oreos with the initial query, the response would have undoubtedly been, "What the hell is *this* all about?"

No question, it's a delicate balance and it's not easy. For that reason, I suggest you read everything you can about queries and business letters. Devote a lot of time to crafting your query. By "a lot of time," I mean days. Weeks if necessary. Then set the draft aside for a few days and reread it as objectively as possible.

Because no matter how you slice it, you're not just asking the publisher to read your manuscript. You eventually want them to buy it, to part with big bucks to transform it into a Real Book That People Will Pay Money For, which must also be marketed and distributed. So you'd darn well better give them serious reasons to go to such effort and expense. And you do this by employing the basic technique of sales. (More scary organ music.)

Sales? Relax... it's not that bad. In a nutshell, all you do is to stress the benefit to the buyer. In the query, you tell them what you've got and why they should want it. Note I did not say you should tell

HUMOR

them your friends think it's good. The biggest mistake made in most product sales is the same one made by writers trying to sell manuscripts. They stress the product's *features* instead of the *benefit* to the buyer. The successful salesperson does the reverse. You understand the writers' axiom to show not tell, don't you? Then you already understand the feature/benefit distinction.

Think about the sales techniques that work on you. Exaggerated claims, pressure, pushiness, or vague exhortations to please buy? Or would you be more inclined to consider a product presented with a succinct, compelling package of reasons on why you'd benefit by purchasing?

When you compose your query, expand in your mind the concept of what your humor manuscript is. Once written, it's no longer a light-hearted romp or collections of hilarious insights. It's now a commodity in search of an investor. Instead of extolling the product's features ("This funny, heartwarming look at cats is really, really funny and heartwarming."), you stress the benefit to the editor ("A recent survey of frequent book-buyers indicates that fully two-thirds of them are cat lovers, which translates to a potential market of eighty million billion.").

[Of course, in order to seem Authentically Businesslike, you'll want to use real statistics. The Statistical Abstract of the United States, put out by the Census Bureau and available on library shelves, has every kind of quirky little statistic you'd need to craft a compelling sales letter.]

For example, in my query letter for my first book, *And How Are We Feeling Today?*, which is a skewed look at surviving hospitals, I pointed out the 35 million people who are hospitalized annually who would welcome a little commiserating humor... not to mention hundreds of thousands of medical professionals, which of course I did. You can almost hear the editor thinking? "35 million times $8.95 equals... Ka-CHING!

Now remember, at this point she does not know if the thing is funny. She does, however, know that if it is, it's a potential money-maker. And because most books do not turn a decent profit, a

Getting Published

reasonable expectation of sales can elicit a request for the manuscript. Had I demonstrated in the query only that I was funny, I may have succeeded in momentarily entertaining her, but that's not sufficient to trigger the salivary response. Nailing the numbers shows you've done your homework and lends instant credibility to your pitch.

Additionally, it's important to research the competition. When I first began *And How Are We Feeling Today?* I assumed that there'd be dozens of humor books on hospitals. Amazingly, there weren't. Existing ones were outdated, out of print, and quite different from mine. You can bet my query pointed that out! If I hadn't done this, perhaps the editor would have assumed as I did that there were a ton of books like mine – and since she couldn't think of any off the top of her head, they probably had lousy sales, so why would she want to do another?

Even if the topic does have strong current competition, you can use that to your advantage by pointing out the huge market that evidently exists to support so many books on the same subject. Then, merely show how yours is different, better, and how the very same market will now come clamoring for yours.

Including marketing info on competition shows you're on top of things; you know how the biz works and you're in the same camp as the editor. You're now not merely a writer, you're an ally. An acquisitions editor's value to the firm is ultimately judged by sales receipts for the books she's recommended for purchase.

Let's see why this is important. Let's say the editor's impressed with the query. Liking the premise of your book, she weighs her workload and, because you've done such a smashing job of research, decides it's worth her time to read the manuscript.

You send it, she reads it. She wants to buy. Hooray! Not so fast there… **Now** she has to convince the rest of the company. Your businesslike approach – your edge – now gives her the edge. Your research gives her solid facts to use when arguing in favor of your book at the acquisitions meeting – a meeting where other acquisition editors have **their** pet manuscripts on the table competing for a slot in the fall catalogue.

HUMOR

To make matters worse, now marketing and financial officers get into the act. What do you think they want to hear? Are they moved by your delicious wit? No, they want numbers, specifically ones with dollar signs. Armed with your research, an editor who loves your work has the ammunition to fight for it.

Whew! By now you've figured out the unglamorous truth that getting published is mostly sloggingly tedious work. That's not to say there aren't prerequisites – you know those pesky little extraneous details like talent and a working command of the language. (I assume you have those prerequisites nailed; not much I can do for you if you don't. This is only one chapter, guys!)

Actually, I'd love to dish out TLC and encourage and nurture any and all aspiring humor writers ('cause I'm just that kinda gal) but fact is, writing for publication is no place for thin skins and tender egos. There are boatloads of people who write funny –some of them even do it deliberately – and they all want to get published. Only a lucky few will succeed.

Lucky? Did I say lucky? Luck has little to do with it. Note that I did not say it had **nothing** to do with it. Luck and chance do play a part. A bazillion arbitrary factors come into play – the editor's mood when your query arrives, her workload, budgets, the last P & L statement, the weather, subway strikes, and for that matter, how she feels about Cool Whip.

Stiff competition and junk beyond your control make it crucial to zero in on things you **can** control. Yes, getting published is a long shot; getting hit by lightning is a long shot too. But it happens! And, Ancient Druid Secret: stroll around a golf course during a thunderstorm wearing metal cleats carrying a five iron. (Don't forget to act like you belong there.)

With writing, talent is your five iron; professionalism and a businesslike approach are your cleats.

Now go crash The Party.

HOW I WRITE A ROMANCE
by Lauren M. Phelps

When you were in grade school, did you ever grow a crystal in a sugar solution? For me, writing a romance novel is like that. Every story is unique, but each starts from a single particle, the germ of an idea that expands and unfolds into a story of two people and their love for one another.

That first idea may not be the novel's heart, may not even play a big part in the finished product. It can be anything – a newspaper article, an old house that catches my eye, a glimpse of a young woman playing with a child. Sometimes I'll jot down a few notes, or toss a clipping into a file, but more often that moment in time will simply settle in my mind, fermenting, raising questions. Who? Why? What if? What if a murder was committed in that old house? What if the young woman had snatched the child from its abusive parents and was hiding from the law?

From this "what if" process, I develop a premise for the book. Perhaps the victim murdered in that old house died right before her wedding and now wants to keep the heroine safe until **her** wedding day. The young woman could meet the hero while searching for a champion to protect the child. At this point I usually begin writing; just a sentence or two, to gel the idea.

Theme comes next. Theme is the "moral of the story" that no one notices, if it's done well. Common romance themes are 'Love Conquers All,' "Love Can't Exist Without Trust," 'Love Will Set You Free." My personal favorite is 'First Love Yourself Before Loving Another." I write my theme down as soon as I identify it.

So far, writing a romance looks very much like writing any other novel, doesn't it? Premise, theme, plot, characters... But wait, I never mentioned plot, and for good reason. Plot is the point at which romance novels differ from other books.

A romance is the story of two people and their relationship. Characters, not plot, drive the book. That's why, before I plot my novel,

Getting Published

I write extensive character sketches for my hero and heroine, shorter ones for secondary characters, even a few sentences for minor characters, if they exist. Often there are no minor characters, especially in contemporary series romances.

I didn't do character sketches at first, but found that I ended up with flat, pale characters who lacked the gumption to complete the tasks I'd set for them. So now I put first things first – character before plot.

The heart of my character sketch is a one-sentence snapshot of my character's soul. "Jean-Marc doesn't know how to trust a woman." "Lara wants a home and family more than anything in the world." "Sheridan's word is his bond."

Next, I explain why this is the very essence of his or her personality: What happened to make Jean-Marc so distrustful, why Lara wants a family so much, how Sheridan came by his high principles. I explore how that main trait plays out in the character's life, and in doing so pin down a whole set of faults and virtues that flow from it. I also develop a history for my character; where she was raised, how she did in school, etc. Physical descriptions appear now, but they're sketchy: "red hair, blue eyes," because they are not important. Everyone looks beautiful through the eyes of the love.

Next comes the conflict. This is easy if I've picked the right characters, because conflict flows from the characters' basic personalities. Take Marianne, an orphan, who spent her childhood in foster homes and so craves stability. Rob's quiet strength wins her heart, but he's an Air Force pilot, and that same strength of character demands that he serve his country by risking his life in strange, unfriendly lands. I'm not happy until I can express my conflict in one sentence: Marianne must choose between her need for stability and Rob's love.

I then fill out a "Standardized Plot Outline," a form I designed using ideas borrowed from Joseph Campbell's *The Hero with the Thousand Faces*, a book every novelist should at least skim. The

ROMANCE

essential idea is that all myths (and by extension, stories) share a similar structure.

Here's my outline:
1. The heroine appears in her normal state.
2. She receives the Call to Adventure (to romance).
3. She resists the Call.
4. She meets her mentor or confidant.
5. Complications and roadblocks arise. (This step will be repeated several times. Each time, she solves the problem, only to be confronted with a worse one.)
6. The Cave. (Here she receives the insight needed to meet the final challenge when she gets to the Crisis.)
7. The Crisis (the black moment). (More complications may arise before the crisis).
8. The Resolution. Here, the heroine grabs for the brass ring, and because this is a romance novel, catches it.
9. The End. All that's left is to tie up the loose ends.

Step 4 can be omitted, but the rest have to be there, though not necessarily in quite this order. If I can fill out my outline to my satisfaction, I move to the next step. If not, I set it aside or look for another idea.

The outline gives me the book's high points. Next, I take those high points and write my synopsis. Why, you might ask, write a synopsis when I don't have even one chapter? Because it's easier. I'm not tied to plot details, so I focus on the central conflict and a couple of great scenes. I'll also use the synopsis as a selling tool.

Finally, I plot my novel, and it's here that romances part company with other stories. This may seem obvious, but in a romance novel, the romance **is the plot**. The action is a subplot. It should intertwine with the romance, but all the critical events take place inside the characters' heads, or between hero and heroine. Rob (the Air Force pilot, remember?) may go to some third world country and shoot up a terrorist, but what's important is how he feels about it, how it affects his relationship with the home-loving Marianne, not the body count.

Getting Published

Because my characters' feelings, their inner turmoil and growth are what really matter, I write an "Emotional Outline." I multiply the proposed number of chapters by expected scenes per chapter (all determined by the reading the kind of books I like to write) and write the scene numbers, say, 1-38, on lined paper.

Then I jot down what my characters are feeling during that scene. I might write, "Scene 1. Marianne meets Rob and is struck by his take-charge manner. Rob finds her tart wit enchanting." If I know that this comes about when he saves her from drowning while everyone else is milling around in panic, I'll put that down, but if not, I don't worry. As long as I know what has to happen inside Marianne and Rob, I feel comfortable.

If I have subplots, I'll outline them, too. A romance subplot gets an Emotional Outline, while an adventure or mystery subplot is handled with a conventional outline. I also like to note where and how the romance and the subplots intertwine.

Only now do I begin writing my romance.

I still don't know everything that's going to happen to my characters, but I know enough. I don't have to worry about writing myself into a corner, or writer's block, or cardboard characters, or extensive, painful editing (which I hate) because my pre-work solved those problems before they even arose. The hard work is behind me.

All that's left is the part I love, the part than I became a writer to do – telling the story of a man and woman in love.

ROMANCE

THE ROMANCE MARKET – AN OVERVIEW
by M. Sue Lemmon

Romance is big business. According to the latest statistics released by the Book Industry Study Group, of all mass market paperbacks sold in the U.S. romance accounted for 48.6% in 1992:

• Romance represented 177 million books sold, for a total sales figure of approximately $885 million. That amounted to a 5.2% increase over 1991, according to *Publishers Weekly*.

• Romance novels are sold in more than 100 international markets and in 26 languages around the world.

• In 1994 Harlequin romances sold 6.8 million copies in Hungary alone.

These are some pretty heady statistics. An aspiring writer of category or series romance should know, though, that his/her book will not be around for extended periods of time. These books have a shelf life of barely three weeks. That is not a long time to make it or break it. While some publishing houses maintain a **back list** of books for some authors – *many do not*. A back list, it should be pointed out, is where reprints come from. In romance, they rarely exist. If you do not purchase your books up front to have for future conferences or book signings, they just might not be available to you – ever. If you purchase a big supply, you may have an inventory of 'yellowed" copies to sell to autograph seekers where you may be presenting a workshop or speaking.

While romance writing and publishing can be very tough worlds, aspiring romance writers, unlike those in other genres, have access to assistance on "How to Write Romance... " through publishers of romance who will furnish editorial guidelines (tip sheets) upon request with an enclosed SASE (self-addressed stamped envelope).

Getting Published

Another way to gather information is through the Romance Writers of America, which also has much to offer would-be writers. RWA is a national writing affiliation of almost 8,000 aspiring and published authors. RWA was established to promote excellence in romance fiction, to help writers become published and establish careers in their writing field, and to provide continuing support for authors within the romance publishing industry.

To accomplish these goals, RWA strives to educate and assist members through an annual conference, a bi-monthly magazine – *Romance Writers Report (RWR)*, annual contests and awards – the RITA for published authors, the Golden Heart for unpublished authors, and through the meetings of local chapters across the nation and around the world.

Like much other genre fiction, romance is based on fantasy and our readers know it. Here are some facts concerning your audience for romance fiction:
- The average romance reader is 39 years of age.
- Forty-five percent are college educated.
- More than 50% work outside the home.
- Their average household income is $40,000.

The appeal of romance novels is as complex as it is powerful. Romance covers the gamut of sensuality from sweet traditional to extremely sensual. Within the publishing houses there may be several lines of romance which include the following: Realistic to fantasy, paranormal – ghosts and vampires, time-travel/futuristic, western, intrigue, and mystery. This includes the short, contemporary and mainstream. The romantic historical may cover many different periods such as regency, cowboy/western, and medieval.

Authors of romance will confirm that you can't write successful romances unless you love to read them first. As Jayne Ann Krentz, noted romance author and the person responsible for compiling and editing *Dangerous Men and Adventurous*

ROMANCE

Women – Romance Writers on the Appeal of the Romance, (University of Pennsylvania Press NEW CULTURAL STUDIES) said, "It is a genre that requires absolute sincerity." She goes on to say that, "... writers who 'drop into' the field with the intention of churning out a few quick books in order to make some fast money rarely last long, if they manage to get published at all. If they are successful in selling a manuscript or two, the resulting books are never the ones that prove most popular with the readers."

Writers of romance must write fantasies that are accessible to their readers. It is not writing "to formula" but rather writing compelling fiction that comes ALIVE. Category or series romance must conform to strict guidelines respecting the basic concept of the genre in that the story must be about a monogamous relationship between two people who grow and overcome internal/external conflicts and become strong and committed to one another by the end of the book. It requires a **guaranteed happy ending** concluding in marriage or a lifetime commitment to one another. And while authors are constantly "pushing the envelope" regarding current mores and trends, the basic concept must hold true.

CHILDREN

CREATING YOUR OWN FOUNTAIN OF YOUTH
by David R. Collins

I watched the girl approach me, her arms holding one of my books, *FLORENCE NIGHTINGALE,* to her chest. In the midst of her full freckled face, a cheerful smile revealed a missing front tooth. "Mr. Collins, I love this book," she said. "It made me want to be a nurse when I grow up."

I thanked the girl profusely, pleased that I had accepted the invitation to visit this elementary school. So many of the kids seemed to have read my books; the school librarian had done her job well. But before I had time to completely bathe in ego juice, another one of the third graders stepped forward. This young man wore no smile at all, and he held a copy of my own *ZACHARY TAYLOR* as if it – if I recall the term from my distant childhood – had cooties.

"I had to read this book," Josh declared, his voice dripped in venom. (I knew his name from his right arm which boasted a rolled up T-shirt and a temporary – I hope it was temporary – tattoo.) "It was the boringest book I ever read."

I nodded. "I appreciate your honesty, Josh," I answered. His face could not hide his surprise at my reaction and his name recognition, and he turned and stumbled back to his seat.

Every published writer for children has his or her own collection of personal memories. Publication of a juvenile magazine story or a children's book makes you an instant celebrity among those teachers and librarians who lead 'the charge of the mite brigade." Whether it's a classroom or library setting, you are subjected to the careful inspection of countless faces, each wondering if you **really** wrote the selection/s they have heard or read. After all, we live in a machine world, and some little people have difficulty accepting the fact that ideas start inside minds not computers.

But that's exactly where ideas do start, and if you have any notion of writing for children successfully, you had better plan to create from a fresh fountain of youth. Boys and girls demand the best! They won't settle for less. Every word must count.

Getting Published

Decide that you are going to entertain and educate in your writing. Yes, think with a "Double E" standard in mind. It is essential since you are writing for young readers, that you make it **E**njoyable. If you make that reader constantly struggle for meaning or understanding, you are going to turn that child off. Shame! Would you deliberately stand in the way of a young person's education or recreational pleasure? I would hope not. When you decide to write for children, whether it be a poem, play, story, article or book, you commit yourself to write with clarity and zest, with spark and enthusiasm.

Don't write down to the reader. Make that young mind reach. If you believe the word **naïve** is just right for your fourth grade story, make sure you provide the meaning through context, i.e., 'Billy was very naïve. He would believe anything anyone told him." No, you don't have to sit with a graded word list in front of you as you write, but you must develop a vocabulary awareness, a sense of what words are familiar to what age child. How to do this? Read lots of their books. Familiarize yourself with basic reading formulas. Talk to librarians and teachers.

Don't overlook the importance of short sentences for the little people. **You** may think in complex and compound-complex sentences. Kids don't. Keep it fast moving and unstilted. Read your material aloud as you write. Children's writing is enhanced by a lyrical flow, a rhythmic beat. No, we're not talking rap – we're simply saying that which **sounds** good to children is often more appreciated. It's essential for tots to whom the material is read aloud. If they like the way something sounds, they will enjoy it more – and understand it better too.

In trying to make your writing for children **E**ducational, the second "e" of your goal isn't to be taken in the dry, dull sense. It means that you realize that you are writing for readers less experienced in living and less familiar with topics. Creating fictional characters and plots which boys and girls can identify with and learn from is an admirable calling. Growing up is not easy, it never has been, and if a writer can provide an easier and less painful way of doing so, then that writer is offering a valuable service.

One can never imagine the impact a story may have on a child. Remember my freckled-faced friend at the beginning of this article? My biography of Florence Nightingale gave her inspiration and direction. Certainly, I know that can and probably will change tomorrow or next week. But for the moment, I touched a stranger's mind and offered hope.

Hope – that's another essential for children's writing. If you want to have your protagonist commit suicide, write for adults. Yes, I know it happens. But young people must not see suicide as an option for problems. Let youth live good old Scarlett's philosophy, that "Tomorrow is another day." Let them also feel that it could be a better day too.

Selecting topics for children to read about is exciting. Dinosaurs have been a favorite of the young for decades, but there are kids interested in polar bears and canaries too. Rivers, the weather, collecting coins, holidays, major sports accomplishments – for every topic, there are readers. They want to know and grow, and you can help them.

It's important when you write for children to aim for an age range. People who write for adults do not have to be so restricting. Generally, professional juvenile writers think 2-5, 6-9, 9-12, and 12-15. The young adult category follows, but many 15+ers are reading adult material. The age for whom you are targeting has a major effect on length and topic. Additional reading in how-to/what-to books and marketing sources is required.

Marketing is a whole new ball game. The late Lee Wyndham often said, "Writing is only half the job – the other half is marketing." Don't worry about agents. Finds markets you feel comfortable with and get to know editors via submission. They're not all monsters; some are actually human. If you have a speck of talent, they will help guide you.

Write for that child within you. To write young, think young. Use the senses in your writing. Let the reader taste, smell, see, hear and touch with your protagonist. Make characters real or fanciful. BE accurate with your non-fiction. Yes, young readers deserve the best.

And if you're so inclined, try a new children's biography about Zachary Taylor. Josh would appreciate it!

Take-Along Guide
Rabbits, Squirrels and Chipmunks

by Mel Boring   illustrations by Linda Garrow

CHILDREN

The Children's Book Market: An Overview
by Mel Boring

Today's market for children's books has come a long way since the Kennedy Administration's everyone-read literacy goal of the early 1960's – a long way *down*. In our most honest moments, we who write for children must be asking: Are kids out there reading anymore? And the honest answer is no, certainly not as many as 40 years ago, maybe not even as many as five years ago. So at the turn of the century, more than ever, we have to "hook" children into reading, with fast-paced, excitingly written, with-it books.

In response to JFK's literacy leadership of the '60's, children's publishers went into overtime and overdrive to flood the country with children's books. But the *coup dètat* of 1963 in Dallas destroyed that literacy drive. And children's publishers were forced into undertime and underdrive; the flood of children's books became a trickle.

During the 1970's, the market for children's writing went so mushy that many of us wondered why we had ever gotten into it anyway. Children's publishers began to restructure for survival. Many famous giants, such as Harper & Row, or Macmillan, became "small fish in the bigger pools" of corporate merger. Multicorps like Gulf Oil even grabbed their way into publishing, buying up Houghton Mifflin, which contained Clarion. All of this up-sizing did result, it must be said, in an increase in the number of children's books produced.

However, for example, Harper's was drowned in HarperCollins. And Simon & Schuster ate up not only Macmillan (which itself swallowed others, like Dillon Books) but Aladdin Paperbacks, Atheneum Books and Margaret K. McElderry Books. So we who submit manuscripts now face huge "conglomerates" where manuscripts are all-but-lost, and even veteran authors are forced to beg for contracts.

Getting Published

A well-published author friend, who has published a hundred children's books during the past quarter-century, wrote recently that he had lost *another* editor, who was laid off by a major *publisher*; and he had lost another publisher, because "the Macmillan Children's Books imprint was killed off by Simon & Schuster." He went on, "I've seen ups and downs before, but this seems worse than usual… This year [1995] will be a real test, since I need several new contracts to keep my enterprise afloat." So languishes the never-lucrative-anyway business of writing for children.

The children's book market resurged in the late 1980's, fueled mainly by "Yuppie" parents who became more active in making sure their children could read. As a result, among the age-range openings in the market, the demand for books for preschool, and even pre-preschool children, grew. And that niche has remained, although it too has been downsized.

The rising output of children's books hit a peak of 5,056 titles in 1990, twice as many as had been published in 1980. In the early 1990's, children's books, which had been a $2.5 billion annual business, had grown to $5 billion. Now, however, the increases of that children's book boom of the 80's are being cut back. During the past five years, the market has gone as soft as a bunny tail.

Many publishers have been taking a hard look at the profitability of their juvenile divisions. Children's editors are being ordered to cut back on the size of their lists by a certain percentage, to delay publication on some titles already in production, and even to cancel existing contracts. Staff positions have been eliminated, and the downsizing is eliminating both books and people, making the editors in children's publishing offices as nervous as long-tailed cats in rooms full of rocking chairs.

I was rudely reminded of the softness of today's children's book market by the rejection of a book which Scientific American Books for Young Readers seemed bound to accept when first submitted a year and a half ago. But today came the editor's rejection letter, saying that they have decided to stop acquiring children's books, period! I will submit it elsewhere, of course; but it reminds me of the many "stops" and "holds" being slammed on our business today.

Another children's author recently held a solid track record at Scholastic, one of the few remaining bastions of children's publishing. But they rejected her next book of the same genre she had been selling in regularly. They then asked if she was interested in writing certain titles they were seeking. But she could not bring herself to produce the kind of market-driven books being sought, such as *The Vampire Who Stole Christmas*.

This is one type that is selling: books of haunting, horror and the hairy-scary. Scholastic's recent R.L. Stine successes with the *Goosebumps* series is one frightening instance. "Frightening," because many such books are thick in blood, but thin in plot, characters and substance. They are exciting to read, but easy to forget. Also selling are any spinoff books from movies like *Aladdin* and *Pocahontas*. But where is the *lasting* children's literature, books that won't blow in – then out with the winds of trends?

They are still around, in the likes of *The Giver* by Lois Lowry, a very deserving winner of the 1994 Newbery Award, and in picture books, such as *If You Give a Mouse a Cookie* and *If You Give a Moose a Muffin*, by Laura Foffe Numeroff. In books like these, children's literature is still alive and *well*. So there is still a way for you to write, and publish, the less fad-oriented, market-driven, and more time-lasting children's books. But the gate is narrow, the way is hard, and writers who find it are few.

One terribly distressing current trend is that more and more children's publishers are refusing even to read unsolicited manuscripts. It is partly the result of all the downstructuring, and

Getting Published

partly because of the increasing mass of unsoliciteds they receive. If you are an already-published author, that might help you get a reading. But because still more publishers are reaching toward agented submissions, the handwriting on the wall for us may say that, in a few years, every children's writer will *have* to have an agent in order to sell anything.

There are a few bright spots in the children's book marketplace, at least for the present, and possibly the future. The first spot is a "large" and the other two "mediums," as measured by the number of books they publish per year.

HarperCollins Children's Books is one children's book publisher that continues to accept and read all unsolicited submissions. They are open to receiving picture books, illustrated chapter books, and fiction and nonfiction for middle-graders and young adults as well.

    HarperCollins Children's Books
    HarperCollins Publishers
    10 East 53rd Street
    New York, NY 10022
    Address Submissions Editor

Boyds Mills Press is only about a decade old, but is noteworthy because of its parent, *Highlights for Children*, one of the longest-established children's magazines. Boyds Mills has focused largely on picture books, although that focus may be shifting, for they produce novels for middle-grade and young adult readers as well. They also do some 10% subsidy-publishing, though nothing about Boyds Mills makes them an easy mark for manuscripts.

    Boyds Mills Press
    Highlights for Children
    815 Church Street
    Honesdale, PA 18431
    Address Beth Troop: Manuscript Coordinator

CHILDREN

Clarion Books, largely because of the influence of long-time former editor, Jim Giblin, and the present editorship of Dorothy Briley, treats authors very considerately. An imprint of Houghton Mifflin Company, Clarion's list includes fiction, non-fiction, and picture books for infants through middle-grade readers.

>Clarion Books
>Houghton Mifflin Company
>215 Park Avenue South
>New York, NY 10003
>Address Dorothy Briley:
>Editor-in-Chief/Publisher

All three of these publishers offer guidelines to help children's writers. If you study them, and write books which follow those guidelines, your market for children's books may go a long way up in the next century. Writing for children used to be called a bunny-eat-bunny world; now it has become dog-eat-dog. But then, children's writing – like old age – is not for sissies.

HOW TO WRITE THE ONLY TRUE AMERICAN GENRE
by Wendi Lee

The American public has always had an on-again, off-again love affair with the western novel. The genre was steadily popular from the 1800's when it first appeared in dime novel form up to 1960 when Louis L'Amour was in his prime. The western began to decline in popularity in the 1970's. Since then, interest in western fiction has usually been dependent on the success of the western in films, television shows, and mini-series. For instance, when the movie *Young Guns* hit the screen in 1988, western fiction enjoyed a jump in sales. This happened again with the *Lonesome Dove* TV mini-series and Clint Eastwood's Oscar®-winning film, *Unforgiven*.

The western can't be set any place else in the world. You can write a romance set in Asia or Australia, a mystery or suspense novel can be set in Istanbul or Idaho, but a true western novel can only be set in the United States during the Westward Expansion, generally between 1840 and 1900.

There are several types of western novels: the traditional western, the novel of the West, the historical western, and the western saga or series. All forms require a good plot and characterization, but there are some differences.

Traditional Westerns

Traditional westerns such as Louis L'Amour's *Hondo* don't require a complex plot. Traditionals rely on plenty of action with a hero who has a strict sense of right and wrong. Traditional western novels aren't set in the real Old West, but in an Old West that exists only in the imagination of the writer.

In the real Old West, morals were a gray area for many of the gunfighters and lawmen. In a traditional western, the gunfighters have strong moral codes and often fight for the rights of the little

Getting Published

guys against the big bad guys. The meek, the poor and the downtrodden shall inherit the earth – if one mean mother who's fast with a gun and has the moral fiber of a schoolmarm can be convinced that it's the right thing to do.

Novels of the West and Historicals

A novel of the West such as Larry McMurtry's *Lonesome Dove* has a literary tone and leans toward mainstream. Novels of the West don't deal in black-and-white plots, and the writer attempts to portray the West as it really was. The main focus is the characters and how they interact. Novels of the West often feature non-traditional protagonists such as a woman or a black man. Recently, there was a trend toward American Indians and mountain men as main characters.

The historical western is usually a large book of 100,000 words plus. An example of a classic historical would be A.B. Guthrie's *The Big Sky*. Set during an important event in western history, numerous characters play out multiple subplots against an expansive background. Customarily, the writer will include historical figures for brief walk-on parts.

In both novels of the West and historicals, plots grow out of the characters and how they deal with both the inner and outer changes of their environment.

Series Westerns

The western saga or series is a very broad subgenre that denotes a group of books that have a common character or characters. The key to a good series is an interesting main character, one who will hold the reader's interest. My traditional western series is about ex-Texas Ranger Jefferson Birch, a drifter who is a part-time private detective.

A series can take many forms – traditional, historical, or the adult western series. Adult westerns are almost always series: several sex scenes and graphic violence usually play a large part in an adult western series. The plot of an adult western series usually follows the traditional western format.

Other Categories

There are two subgenres: short stories and young adult novels. Currently, the western short story can be found in only two places: *Louis L'Amour's Western Magazine*, published bimonthly by Dell Magazines, and western anthologies, which are published at the whim of the publisher.

The young adult western is usually between 25,000 and 35,000 words long. Although good plotting and characterization apply here as well, readers between the ages of ten and fifteen don't like to read the same sort of story as adults do. Plot grows out of how the main character, a young adult like the reader, resolves conflicts and relates to others.

Research

Louis L'Amour once said in an interview that he did research for his books to make the West come alive for his readers.

Whether you're writing about the real or the mythical Old West, research is an important tool. I have a modest library of books and have found that the ones I use the most are as follows: *The Looks of the Old West* by Foster-Harris; *The Historical Atlas of the American West* by Beck and Haase; *Rand McNally's Pioneer Atlas of the American West, Story of the Great American West* edited by Reader's Digest; *The Writers' Guide to Everyday Life in the 1800's* by Marc McCutcheon; and *The Book of the American West* edited by Jay Monaghan. Most of these books are out of print and hard to find, but by haunting used book stores, library book sales, and antique malls, I've managed to create a well-stocked library.

If you find a copy of *The Look of the Old West*, hang onto it. This book tells you how long it took by train, horse, and wagon to cross the American West. It tells you what someone would wear

Getting Published

and what they would carry with them, the different parts of a saddle, what the most common guns were, what a soldier wore as opposed to a civilian, and many more essential facts.

The Writers' Guide to Everyday Life in the 1800's is still available through Writer's Digest Books, and gives the writer obscure facts about slang and everyday language, popular food and drink, money and coinage, courtship and marriage rituals and more.

The Historical Atlas of the American West is, as far as I know, still in stock and would be an important addition to your library. Published by the University of Oklahoma Press, this atlas covers the West from Montana to Texas and beyond, and information ranges from the different railroad and stagecoach routes to the average daily temperature in January and June to the military forts from 1819 to 1895. It shows you the commonly traveled cattle routes, field crops, gold and silver bonanzas, Indian lands, important battles of the Civil, Mexican, and Indian wars, and more.

Books on Native Americans, the way they lived, their medicines, their folklore, should also line your shelves. I also recommend children's books on the West. These books will tell you things that adult books will leave out because the information is too common to the adult western scholar. Since I have no pretensions of being a scholar of the Old West, I am happy to buy children's editions of western history, railroad history, and the history of western states such as Oregon, Utah, or Nevada.

Western fiction is probably one of the most unstable genres in category fiction, but if you enjoy reading it and aspire to write it, we will always keep the West, mythical and real, alive.

AN OVERVIEW OF THE MARKET FOR WESTERNS
by Vince Matthews

Those of us who write westerns have seen our share of the markeplace enjoy a mild resurgence during the mid 90's. In the 70's, we seemed to have gone the way of the Native American and the covered wagon. As Wendi Lee pointed out in her piece, since that time the genre has ridden various waves of popularity depending more and more on what America's taste in movies happens to be.

Westerns, like most genre writing, is cyclical. Horror, true crime, and several others have had swings in popularity as well. Right now, there seems to be a small upswing again in westerns. Though the number of publishers is dwindling, the ones who still publish westerns are interested in a strong story with full-rounded characters. I have heard of one publisher who haunts art shows, buys western art which he uses for his covers, then commissions a writer to write a novel that reflects the art he has purchased. But most of them are still interested first by the story the writer has to tell.

Most westerns selling today fall into one of two categories, at least from a marketing standpoint. The adult western series predominates in paperback sales, while more traditional westerns, published in hardback, are for library sales. The only exception to this being hardback sagas, such as Larry McMurtry's *Lonesome Dove*, which find their way onto the mainstream shelves.

The market is tight, but there are still places for westerns to find a home. Let's hope there always will be.

MYSTERY

THE MYSTERY OF WRITING MYSTERIES
by Max Allan Collins

No formula exists for writing a mystery novel. In fact, no working definition even seems to exist – many a "mystery" (most Robert B. Parker novels, for example) don't have a mystery or puzzle element at all, anymore. These days, what I think of as a crime novel or perhaps an action or adventure novel is funneled into the mystery genre, and what are you going to do about it?

But for the sake of discussion, let's assume a mystery **does** have a mystery element – that is, a crime (usually but not always a murder) to be solved by a protagonist who is either an amateur or professional detective. What makes novels of mystery or crime so compelling to both reader and writers is that such a novel inherently contains a conflict – crime and murder being by definition products of human conflict – and conflict is the engine of any **real** story.

So the crime – and its solution – are central to a mystery novel. The crux. The be-all-and-end-all.

Not necessarily. Alfred Hitchcock called the mystery element (frequently, the object or data or whatever the bad guy and/or his protagonist are pursuing) the "MacGuffin," a nonsense word suggesting that the engine of the story was just an excuse for the interesting characters and colorful incidents that were built around it.

I would disagree with my favorite filmmaker only to the extent that the solution of a truly satisfying mystery should illuminate the entire story. When Sam Spade accuses the bad guy (actually, girl) at the end of the greatest mystery novel ever written, *The Maltese Falcon*, light gradually permeates the dark and mysterious places of the narrative that have preceded his chilling confrontation. We learn not only the details of who killed who and why – we learn the true nature of several key characters in the novel, including the detective himself.

Getting Published

Though a great plot technician, Dashiell Hammett cared more about character than plot; and Raymond Chandler, one of Hammett's few true peers, often said a good mystery novel was one you'd read even if the last page was missing.

So the best piece of advice I can give aspiring mystery novelists is to worry less about the mystery and more about the novel. A mystery novel is first and foremost **a novel**. Modern readers expect rich, interesting, believable characters in vivid settings; readers also appreciate social commentary, and it's been said that you can learn more about an era by reading its best mystery writers than by reading that era's most respected literary lights. John D. MacDonald and Ed McBain are especially good in this regard.

This is true whether you wish to walk down Chandler's mean streets or enter Agatha Christie's cozy parlors. Readers expect more than just a puzzle. They will put up with no puzzle at all, if the story itself – which is to say the characters and the incidents that grow out of those characters' interactions – is compelling.

As to setting, I would suggest using one you are familiar with. The trend over the past 10 or 15 years has been for authors to stake out some territory as their own. From the biggest city to the smallest bump-in-the-road village, crimes occur and interesting people can be involved with them. I have used my hometown, Muscatine, Iowa (as "Port City") but I've also written extensively about Chicago in the 30's and 40's. So-called regional mysteries attract readers in the given region, of course, but even more so, outside of that region. Readers like both the familiar and the unfamiliar.

I would suggest avoiding overloading your detective – whether a professional or amateur – with too many gimmicks. Don't confuse schtick with characterization. A nun with an eye-patch, a pet penguin and a Watson who happens to be a gay midget theatrical agent just might be overdoing it a tad.

Also, setting out overtly to create a series character is probably a mistake. Most of the great series detectives were one-shot characters by writers who sat down meaning only to write one really terrific novel. Don't try to write a good series, write a great book and maybe you'll be asked to write another. There will be no book number two about Sister Mary Eye-Patch, her penguin and her gay pal Gus A. Levine if book number one doesn't fly.

Mickey Spillane claims to write his last chapters first. By writing the scene in which Mike Hammer explains to the villain how he (Mike) figured out the mystery, Mickey creates what is essentially the synopsis of the book. You should know who did it, and why. You should know where you are headed. You don't have to create a detailed outline, necessarily; you don't absolutely have to take a road map along on your trip. Sometimes it's more fun to take side trips and go adventuring, after all.

But you do need to know where you are going. And the mystery writer who assembles a large cast of characters without knowing who among them is the killer is casting himself or herself as the social director on the Titanic.

I assume if you want to write mysteries that you love to read mysteries. So my final word of wisdom is for you to re-read some of your favorite mysteries not as a reader, but as a writer – read the novels analytically. Take notes. Study first and last lines of chapters. Good narrative writing is 90% strategy – figure out what, say, Sue Grafton's strategy is in her latest novel. Where do scenes begin and end? How many characters does she use, when and how does she introduce them? Study successful writers like Sue, but don't imitate them; if you do imitate them, don't imitate the surface of the writing – imitate the structure, the underlying craft, that such writers inevitably have mastered.

And, of course, you'll need to rush out and buy two or three of my novels, immediately, for close study. After all, unless you do, you won't know whether or not my advice is worth taking. No mystery in that.

HOW WE WRITE TRUE CRIME
by Pat Gipple & Matthew V. Clemens

True crime presents unique and varied problems for the fledgling author. The most difficult part of this genre is to understand that someone has had to suffer, usually had to pay the ultimate price, for you to have something to write about. The people you will be dealing with are victims with gaping wounds, police officers who have a difficult job, and criminals who have committed horrible crimes. It is not a genre for the meek.

We have, as a species, a certain macabre fascination with the troubles of other people. That's why traffic always slows around a grisly car wreck, and it's why the Simpson trial enthralled the television viewers of this country. This is your market. It takes strong nerves, and usually a stronger stomach, to succeed.

Those things said, let's deal with some of the specifics of the genre. When you sit down to write the next *In Cold Blood* or *Fatal Vision*, you will be presented with one of two problems concerning research about your particular crime. There will either be very little information available or there will be too much.

The first problem is far less prevalent in The Information Age than it was even 20 years ago. The second concern, which is what we faced with *DEAD WATER*, can be equally daunting. When we started doing research for the book, we were astounded by the amount of material available to us: Transcripts of two trials (each about 1500 pages), pre-trial depositions from the witnesses called to testify, copious notes taken by the investigating officers, videotaped interviews between the police and potential witnesses, 14 six-hour videocassettes of the first trial, as well as all the articles that appeared in three different newspapers over the two year period from the disappearance of the victim until the conviction of her killer.

Getting Published

It was a lot of material. Our dilemma then became what to leave out and what to include. Information culled from your research will fall into distinct categories.

1. Crucial Information. This is any material that deals directly with the crime and its repercussions.

2. Necessary Information. This is background information the reader needs to become familiar with the characters and settings. For us this came in the shape not only of location but of time period. The crime in *DEAD WATER* took place 12 years before the book's publication. We felt obligated to explain the difference in economic conditions in the area where the crime took place. The fact that the area was undergoing an economic depression in 1983 and that the killer was well-off when most of the residents weren't may have entered into the jurors' minds or it may not have, but we still felt that it was information the reader needed to be grounded in the time and place of the crime.

3. Fun Facts. These are things that the writer thinks are bizarre, or cool, or interesting, but have no relevance to your story. These should only be included if they advance characterization. We included the story of the killer receiving a new Corvette from his parents as a high school graduation present. That had no relevance to the crime itself but it did show the character of the killer; that he had been spoiled as a child and also for most of his adult life. In short, it helped round out the character for the reader. In comparison, one of these fun facts that we left out of the book was a poem the killer had scrawled on a recipe card. It was a disturbing, hateful poem that the jurors never saw. It may have helped convince the police that they were on the right track, but it was never presented as evidence in the trials, and we ended up leaving it out because in the big picture it had nothing to do with the book.

So, after six months of research, we felt ready to write the first word of the book though we still had unanswered questions. Which led us to the next dilemma, interviews.

TRUE CRIME

A warning here. Interviews are part of the genre. If you have difficulty talking to people or with being confrontive – you need to get over it. Although research takes the most time, interviews can be a very difficult and necessary part of writing true crime.

One of the reasons for writing in this genre deals with the emotions surrounding a particular crime. These can range from the public outcry raised by a crime or a verdict; the emotions of victims, friends, family, convicts, people who feel they have been unjustly accused... well, you get the idea. Emotions are messy things. The killer in our book turned us down flat when we requested an interview with him so we didn't have to deal with that. The police officers involved still become emotional when discussing the case, as does the prosecutor who was responsible for the conviction. The most difficult interview, though, was with the victim's best friend. This woman had been close to the victim for a decade before the crime and it had been 12 years since the murder, yet she still spent most of our two-hour interview in tears.

It was unpleasant for her and for us; however, because of this woman's courage and grace, we were far better equipped to present a victim we had never met as a three-dimensional person – a woman with feelings, desires, dreams, and fears. The interview process can be difficult, but this is where the basis for characterization comes from.

Get a tape recorder. Tape all interviews no matter how insignificant they may seem at the time. You want to be accurate when you write the book and you don't want some malcontent to sue you after your book hits *The New York Times* bestseller list, claiming that you misquoted what he/she said.

In a lot of ways, the writing of a true crime book is very similar to writing a novel. The reader needs to be firmly grounded in the setting. This ties in to the research portion of true crime from the standpoint that you need to know as much about the settings involved in your book as you do the people. Since *DEAD WATER* was about the discovery of a torso in the Mississippi River, we checked weather reports from 1983 to get temperatures, weather

Getting Published

conditions, river levels and prevailing currents. We interviewed the local Corps of Engineers to find out whether the rollers on the lock and dam were open or closed.

The be-all-and-end-all of this is – WRITE WELL.

As with any genre, good writing sells. A good story has believable, interesting characters that a reader can empathize with. It has conflict. It has a resolution and there is always a hook of some kind. In true crime you have the built-in hook of dealing with something that really happened.

For true crime to really sell, though, it requires something more and these extra hooks come in many varieties: Brutality such as Richard Speck killing seven nurses in an apartment, a serious psychopath like Manson or Gacy, intrigue or politics as in the Von Bulow affair, a question of guilt or innocence similar to *Fatal Vision*, someone famous like O.J., or some other twist.

Do your research, be true to the characters, ground your reader in the setting and write the story as well as you can.

We'll see you in the courtroom.

TRUE CRIME MARKET OVERVIEW
by Matthew V. Clemens

You would have thought the O.J. Simpson murder case would have been a boon to the true crime market. In fact, the reverse seems true. Now only the extremely high profile cases, Simpson and Menendez, seem able to find their way onto the shelves.

It seems like a long time since books like *Fatal Vision, The Minds of Billy Milligan,* and *Buried Dreams* (Tim Cahill's brilliant Gacy book) have been on the shelves with regularity. Such is the nature of the publishing industry. What goes around, comes around, and sooner or later true crime will again begin to sell.

In the meantime, those of us who write in the genre are finding it increasingly hard to find editors who are interested in the less famous cases that many of us cut our teeth on as readers.

As with any sort of writing, the key is perseverance. If this is the market where you choose to write, there are still a few publishers interested in getting these books to the public.

HOW I WRITE TECHNO-THRILLERS
by R. Karl Largent

During a conversation with my publisher 10 years ago when I sold my first novel, my publisher casually mentioned that up until he offered me a contract, he had been looking for a new "horror writer."

"Horror writer?" I repeated, "... you mean you consider my book – the one you just bought – a horror book?"

"That's the way I see it," he said, "and that's the way we'll market it."

And that, fellow authors, is how I became a "horror" writer. I never intended to write in that genre, that's just the way it happened. One of the age-old facts of life in the publishing business is this: when you sell your first book it "slots" you and that's how you are viewed until you get the opportunity to break out of that genre. Having said that, let's move on.

After delivering 10 books, all "horror," on schedule, some of which were my idea and some the product of my editor's fertile imagination, we had a solid business relationship. (Publishers are looking for authors who meet deadline and produce "follow on" books).

That business relationship resulted in a call from New York one day and one of the editors saying, "Karl, have you ever thought of doing a techno-thriller?"

"No," I said. Then I admitted that I had not only not thought about it, I also admitted that I didn't even know for certain what he was talking about.

"I'm looking for a story heavy on technology: bombs, doomsday devices, supersonic aircraft, political intrigue, that sort of thing – the kind of stuff Tom Clancy and Stephen Coonts write." Then he added, "Modern day James Bond stuff. Want to think about it?"

And that's exactly what I did. I thought about it – for two, maybe three weeks before I called him back and told him I would

Getting Published

like to give it a try. We briefly discussed one or two possible story lines, and he instructed me to give him a three or four page synopsis of the developed idea. And that's how I started writing techno-thrillers.

So much for history. Now let's talk about the mechanics of writing in the techno-thriller genre. First of all, they are not 'Rambo" books. The stories require a great deal more development than one bloody action scene after another. Secondly, there are a whole bunch of technocrats out there who are just waiting for you to do something really dumb in your weapons development, even more insane with your submarine, or something completely impossible with the particular aircraft your hero is flying. In other words, you should possess a fairly good idea of the concepts that make modern technology work (especially as it relates to weapons and weapons systems).

Did I understand weapons technology when I started writing techno-thrillers? No way. But I did have a couple of things going for me. One, I had spent four years in the Air Force as a Weather Officer with second seat time in the aircraft of the day. Second, in the process of pursuing a graduate degree years later, I chose to write about a number of things that were "difficult" to explain – and, even though it is immodest to say so, did rather well at it. My writing instructor at the time, Steve Hollander of Indiana University, even expressed the opinion that, after reading some of my efforts, I might have made a better technical writer than a novelist.

His comments, perhaps intended to accomplish other things, nevertheless gave me the confidence to try a techno-thriller even though I readily confess to being the type who can mismanage the simple task of changing a light bulb.

Armed with a story line that required considerable knowledge about the Navy, DSRVs, political assassinations, and the sabre rattling that precedes momentous events like a Third World War, I started doing my research. And that led to my first discovery,

TECHNO-THRILLERS

techno-thrillers require lots and lots (underline the word lots) of research – far more than I ever had to do for my earlier horror novels. For *Red Tide*, my first effort in the techno-thriller genre, I read four resource books on Russia, two on the KGB and GRU, two books on the Kremlin and its inner workings, several NATO studies of Russian weapons, and two different Russian guide books, one of which delved quite deeply into Russian culture. The rest of my research consisted of watching nearly 45 hours of video tapes that focused on both the political intrigue and philosophy of the Communist Party.

In addition, I read Stephen Coonts' *Final Flight*, Tom Clancy's *The Hunt for Red October*, and Martin Cruz Smith's *Gorky Park* and *Polar Star* to get the feel for a subject that only a novel can render. Total research time, almost five months. (This is consistent with Clive Cussler's statement that good research will usually take six to nine months.)

Finally, feeling that I had a handle on my research, I started to lay out my story line. After looking at the story line from several different perspectives, I decided on one that dealt with political events in both Washington and Moscow that impacted events taking place in Negril, Jamaica. The upshot of this was I had to deal with three different time zones. I was constantly juggling whether or not an event that took place in Jamaica could be relayed to Moscow (it's the middle of the night in one place... and forenoon in another) or whether the protagonist or antagonist would be awake to receive the information. The "time issue" became so confusing that I ended up constructing regional time charts (there are nine in Russia alone) just to get the times of certain events correct.

Time, location, and cultural considerations aside, techno-thrillers present authors with two other up-front and significant hurdles that must be overcome in the planning stage. The first is characters and the second is language differences.

The typical techno-thriller (because you are developing more than one story at a time) requires many characters. Why? Because you are working (and converging) two and sometimes three

Getting Published

plots concurrently – plots that must culminate in one climax which is another way of saying you are telling several stories simultaneously (a much more complicated task than introducing sub-plots which are solved as a straight-line story progresses). Multiple plot scenarios require characters to populate each story line. In *Red Tide*, I had 31 Russian characters, seven Jamaicans, and 19 Americans... and I had to develop character profiles for most of them since there were few tertiary characters (by definition, in and gone) in this work. Most of the characters in *Red Tide* were woven in and out of the work several times.

Another often sticky consideration is working the foreign language of the host country (Russian in *Red Tide* and *Red Ice* – and Chinese in *Red Skies*) into your dialogue. How much is enough? When is it appropriate? An occasional italicized Russian or Chinese word can be worked into narrative quite easily. But if the writer is not fluent in a foreign language, working foreign words into dialogue presents the writer with all kinds of problems. How is the word or expression altered by tense, gender, dialectical differences? (It is estimated there are no less than 137 dialects in China – and even more in India.)

On the other hand, the techno-thriller, while difficult to construct because of the techno-problems, probably presents the storyteller with as rich a soup of characters, situations, and possibilities as a multi-generational novel – but condensed into a much shorter time frame. *Red Tide* takes 72 hours to unfold. *Red Ice* takes seven days, *Red Skies* five days. This kind of time frame enables you to set (construct) an almost machine-gun like pace to your story – while at the same time challenging you to find a way to ever accelerate that pace as the story builds to the climax.

The tools of the writer of a techno-thriller are the maps (Moscow, Beijing, or wherever your multiple story lines are set), lists of hotels, restaurants, types of automobiles, sequential ranks of military (a Captain is a big hitter in the Navy, but in the Air Force his equivalent is a Colonel), types of weapons, foods, etc. To facilitate this demand for constant reference material, before I even start a techno-thriller, and after I have "place" nailed down, I head for the nearest used book store, garage or rummage sale, and flea market to sift through the mountains of books that will make ready (and inexpensive) sources and reference material. I find this practice to be less time-consuming than trying to track down some almost incidental (but important) fact on the telephone when I'm actually writing.

Another thing I need to mention about writing a techno-thriller is the need to develop a knack for seeing (or imagining) what the next generation or evolution in a particular kind of technology is going to bring. If you are the kind who could have looked at a 45 rpm record 50 years ago and imagined the evolution of music marketing up through the various tape formats, CDs, to the present day laser discs, you could just as easily have seen the impending evolution of tube technology to transistors, through thin film devices, to the present-day chips. Computers, communications, weapons systems, aircraft – and the ways to destroy them – have proliferated at an even more accelerated rate.

There is some risk in writing a techno-thriller. You must always keep in mind the time frame to produce and publish a book. In most cases we are talking a 30 month turn-around from the time you start the novel until it appears on a news stand. A lot can happen in 30 months. For example, the Soviet Union disintegrated while I was writing *Red Tide*. The novel had to be completely restructured – resulting in a six month rewrite.

Still – techno-thrillers can be fun and profitable. Even more exciting is the news that the market is hungry for them. Write a good one – and you'll have no trouble getting it published.

THE POETS VIEW
by Glenna Glee

Poets are unique in many ways. They cry at parades, are mesmerized at colorful sunsets, and pause to reflect on conversations with cab drivers. The differences continue when it comes to marketing their work. Unless one is already established as a 'known" poet, doors seem to close at the mention of their name, or the word 'poetry."

Poetry has been discontinued by most magazines that once used it regularly. The ones continuing to use poetry have cut down on the numbers and space. Newspapers hardly know it exists. The only remaining outlets for poets are the many small poetry publications and magazines who are willing to publish your work if you subscribe. There are a few prestigious poetry publications that are very difficult to break into. The small publications have an advantage, in that you do manage to get your work and name seen by other poets, and you may be selected by the editor as a featured poet. Each of these small perks is a step forward.

There are probably more amateur poets in the world than all other hobby enthusiasts combined. Some never come out of the closet. Those that do achieve different levels of success and make the competition a bit more challenging.

Most poets eventually become affiliated with local poetry or writing clubs, State Federations, and then with the National Federation. Through these involvements, they learn new forms, read their work to each other and receive feedback, and enter contests, whereby they gain expertise in the craft. When they realize a bit of success, the desire for personal publication arises.

The people they meet in these organizations are very supportive and willing to help in any way. They learn that there are several types of publication, and each enhances the possibility of marketing their work in more desirable places.

Several years ago, I attended the Midwest Writers Workshop in Muncie, Indiana, where Dr. Lee Pennington, Professor at Jefferson Community College in Louisville, and published poet, taught a class in beginning poetry.

Getting Published

Though I had been writing poetry for years, I had had no formal instruction, so I decided this was the place for me. He told our class that any one of us could be published if we were willing to work. He suggested that we put four of our neatly typed poems, one to a page, in envelopes and send them to three publications listed in the *Poets Market* or other source. This was to be done every day of every week for an entire year. Different poems must be sent to each editor. The same poems must never to be sent to two editors at the same time. Good records were to be kept and self-addressed, stamped envelopes included in each mailing for the convenience of the editor. As they returned, if still in good condition, they could be sent to the next place. If they became torn or soiled even slightly, they were to be replaced with new copies. Neatness counts.

I was willing to work, so I took him at his word and gave the system a try. I altered the system slightly; I only sent three mailings a day for five days a week. My results were very good. I had 109 poems published that year. I received very little money, some copies of the publications in which my work appeared; but nonetheless, I knew publishing was possible. It was really up to me.

It is very important that you match your poetry to the publication to which you are submitting. Each editor has special tastes. It is advisable to obtain a copy of the product and study it to find out what type of poetry they use. The listings in the *Poets Market* usually state what type is wanted and how many poems they are willing to see at one time. Address your correspondence to the editor if the name is listed. Query letters are seldom desired for poetry.

Some editors use nothing but free verse, some only want rhymed, some only humor, and some only four-six lines. A few editors will even require poetry on a given subject.

The poet must familiarize himself with the publication and submit something that has a chance. Publication is not an easy task. You must persist and cultivate a very thick skin. The rejections will come; they are a part of the writer's life.

When the poet decides on a book of his own, there are many more lessons to be learned. Self-publication is not an easy task. Some of us never get past that stage. The most simple form of self-publication is the chapbook which is usually prepared by the poet himself. The requirements for this are the ability to type or computerize clear and precise original copy that is then reproduced at a local quick-print facility. The price per book done in this manner can be kept between one and two dollars depending on the number of pages. These chapbooks are usually 5½" x 8½" with a heavier paper used for the cover. Some people make 8½" x 11" books. Either may be stapled in the center or coil bound.

Of course, a far nicer book may be produced by your local printer who does typesetting and perfect binding. It will be more expensive but probably easier to sell. There are also well known subsidy publishers where you pay for the production of your book. Hardback, if desired, will be still more expensive, harder to sell because of the price, and will probably end up in the corner of your bedroom or garage. Subsidy publishers do very little to help market your book.

There are many legitimate opportunities for recognition in poetic circles. One of the major competitions is the Walt Whitman Award, sponsored annually by the Academy of American Poets. It is open to all poetry as well as book-length manuscripts. The winners receive a nice honorarium and a number of published books.

The National Federation of State Poetry Societies is also conducting an annual chapbook contest. There are other opportunities such as these.

An aspiring poet, even a very good one, has a rough way to go. It seems that we poets are the Rodney Dangerfields of the literary society; we get NO respect! It doesnt get better.

My advice to poets would be to flood the editors' desks where poetry is still published. Try to get your work before the eyes of as many people as possible. Hope for the miracle that you can put yourself in demand. The more successful you are in getting published in newspapers, newsletters, church bulletins, magazines, or anywhere, the easier it will be to sell your chapbooks, and to eventually get published by a major publishing house.

When putting your book together, check out the other poetry books in bookstores and the library. Check how they group subject matter and different forms. Model your book after the ones that please you most. Do it! Good luck!

NEWSPAPERS

WHAT I LOOK FOR IN A GOOD (WEEKLY) NEWSPAPER ARTICLE
or
HINTS FROM THE EDITOR FROM HELL
by Viv Sade-Rosswurm

Writing for a weekly newspaper can be a great springboard for showcasing your writing ability, but don't assume because a paper is small, the standards are lower.

For the past six years, I have been a weekly columnist and editor of a small newspaper in my hometown of Churubusco, Indiana. After reading just one article and talking to the author, I can usually tell if it's something our newspaper or maybe our sister newspaper, the *Albion New Era*, would be interested in.

Both newspapers have a circulation of about 2,100 each and publish every Wednesday with deadline on Monday at 5:00 p.m. The papers normally run 20-24 pages, six columns across, and are tabloid size. They sell for $17.50 for a one-year subscription or 40 cents each from the newsstand.

Although our paper is packed every week and we use very few "filler" articles, I would definitely find room for a new, promising article or column *if* I was convinced it was something that would interest our subscribers.

When submitting material, you should be aware of the problems editors run into when considering proposed articles or columns. Some of the most common ones are:

- duplication
- poor grammar and spelling
- unprofessional copy
- articles that are much too long
- articles that do not fit our region and community
- articles written by someone who must be constantly reminded of the writer's guidelines set up by our publishing company.

Getting Published

Duplication

On duplication all I can say is research, research, RE-SEARCH. If you plan to submit an article or a column idea to a local or weekly newspaper, pick up a copy of the paper for two or three weeks prior to submitting your material, and study the contents.

What should you know about the newspaper before you submit an article/column?

Well, first of all, it's good to know the editor's and publisher's names. The reason is twofold: first of all, the editor/publisher will be impressed when you know their name and pronounce it correctly, and secondly, it always helps to know their name when you need to "kiss up."

In no way am I recommending "kissing up," but admittedly, there will be times when this technique might come in handy. But I'm getting ahead of myself – more on that later.

Know the "right" names, know the type of people who live in that geographical area, and know what type of material (columns and stories) they are currently running.

It's more than a little embarrassing to trot into a newspaper office with several sample "gardening tips" columns, only to have the publisher tell you the newspaper has been running a gardening tips column for the *past 20 years*.

If you have something to offer that you feel is similar, but better, than the material currently published, be prepared to explain your reasoning to the editor.

Also be aware that the editor does a lot of the writing, so the article you may be trying to convince the editor "to lose" may, in fact, be HIS or HER column. (This might be one of those cases where you want to refer back to that "kissing up" thing.)

Spelling and Grammar

As a writer, you should know these two subjects are very important areas of consideration given to incoming material.

NEWSPAPERS

If this is news to you, perhaps you should seriously consider a career move.

If a column or article is submitted to one of our newspapers that needs a lot of "cleaning up," otherwise known as "editing," guess who gets it? That's right, the editor. Now I know some of you are sitting out there surmising, "but isn't that an editor's job?" So I just want to clear this up once and for all – yes and no.

Yes, it is one of the editor's jobs to edit material (go figure), but when it becomes too time-consuming to clean up someone's article, well, we tend to get a little testy. And when we get testy, we begin to start looking for other, grammatically correct, precisely-written articles that could fill the space just as nicely. Thus, that other popular phrase, "editor from hell," comes to mind.

The editor who has to clean up your material will eventually find themselves thinking: "I'm not getting any credit for this article, even though I'm practically rewriting it. So why am I busting my chops to make this illiterate slob look good?" And eventually, the editor will eliminate that writer from the personnel files. One thing is very true of all "editors from hell" – they eliminate people who make their job harder.

So before you submit ANYTHING, use a dictionary, get copies of Strunk and White's *The Elements of Style*, and Margaret Shertzer's *The Elements of Grammar*, and READ THEM, run your material through Spellcheck, and get it proofread. In short, do whatever is necessary to make sure the final copy you submit looks polished and professional.

Admittedly, you can get away with poor presentation and preparation much more with our type of publication, a weekly newspaper, than you could with, say, a large daily newspaper, magazine, or periodical.

But, the fact remains – if your work is costing the editors too much time and effort, you will eventually be replaced by someone who is not "high maintenance."

Getting Published

Too Long

I wish I could tell you a magical, acceptable length on all articles, but there really is no set rule and all publications have different specifications. For our newspapers, (a 20-24 pages, 6 columns across, tabloid size) I suppose their "perfect" length would be about 20 column inches, or roughly 500 words. Most of the columns in our papers run between 400 and 600 words.

Being called "editor" at a small, weekly newspaper is really a glorified title, because most weekly editors do it all: the interviews, the stories, the photographs (some even develop their own prints, although I try to bow out of the darkroom as much as possible), the photo captions, the page-layout, the paste-up, and some have even been known to sell the ads and deliver the papers, when necessary. This is in addition to the job of actually "editing" the newspaper, so when it comes time to paste up or lay out the paper, and a column is too long, guess what the editor does? That's right, they CUT it.

Although I usually try my best to fit the entire column in the paper, if I have a particular writer who has been giving us fits by ALWAYS turning in excessively long material, even after being told of the problem, then I probably (this is off the record) go out of my way to cut that particular column. And I never cut the part that the author would choose to cut if they were told to shorten the article. I've been told, usually by the irate writers themselves, that I not only cut the beginning and end of the story, but the focal point, as well.

So save yourself some headaches and stick to the recommended length. Your material is much more likely to stay in one complete piece when it is published.

And while we're talking about this touchy subject – this is probably a good time for me to mention that you really should try and resolve any conflicts you may have with your editor as quickly, and diplomatically, as possible. That's because – and I'm letting you in on a big, inside secret here – the more the editor likes you and your writing, the higher the chance of your material getting published INTACT. Be aware, though, that there are many instances where a piece simply has to be cut; there's no other solution. Don't take it too personally.

"Sorry – doesn't meet our needs"
or
Know the Region and Community

OK, let's say you have a wonderful idea for publishing a column on "Financial Advice and Strategies for Gays and Lesbians in the 90's." Perhaps if you live along the pacific Coast Highway, you'd have little problem marketing this type of column, but I'm here to tell you it would be a mighty hard sell in Poplar Bluff, Missouri. You would probably be shown the front door faster than you can spell "r-e-j-e-c-t-e-d," even if the editor happened to be gay. Why? Because editors and publishers must cater to the tastes and needs of their readers. This, unfortunately, is the hardest concept for most writers to grasp, and the reason so much material is rejected.

Believe it or not, the phrase "this does not currently meet our needs" does NOT translate, in that strange editor/publisher lingo to: "You're a lousy writer, don't ever contact us again;" "Keep the day job;" "I didn't even open the envelope, I just know we won't like it;" or "Have you ever considered a career in mud wrestling?" It really means exactly what it says – IT DOES NOT CURRENTLY MEET OUR NEEDS. But don't give up. Instead, try marketing it to another publication, or revamping the angle of the story so it will meet that particular publication's needs.

Be aware of what type of material the newspaper is running on a regular basis. The editor will have a good feel for what the public wants; they can be a big help to you in that area. Don't be afraid to ask them. A small, weekly paper can be an excellent "foot-in-the-door" for the budding writer, as well as a creative outlet and more exposure for a well-established writer.

Getting Published

For instance, the "Years Ago" column that runs every week in our paper is written by the office manager, who swears she has no writing talent whatsoever. Yet her column is one of the most popular ones we run, especially among senior citizens. All the author does is research old newspapers in this area and write down the highlights of what was going on five, ten, 25 and 50 years ago. This type of column is usually well read and most editors will make room for such an article.

Many times newspapers are forced to run material they may not consider to be especially well-written or interesting, but the public likes it.

For instance, I try not to use the "dirt filler," such as bankruptcy notices, divorce decrees granted, jail bookings, etc., but I won't argue with the fact that the general public likes this stuff, and many newspapers use it as filler.

We are located in a rural conservative area, so 4-H and agriculture are big news. We carry a lot of photos and stories on local 4-H fairs and clubs. Right now, we do not have any type of agricultural column, although I would surely go for it if a writer approached me with such an idea. This is also Amish country, and one Amish lady has cashed in on this with a popular "Amish Tips and Recipe Column" that runs in quite a few weekly and daily papers in Northeast Indiana.

So, look around and know the territory. Make sure the material you submit is something that will appeal to the readership of that particular paper.

"Oops, I forgot about the copyright law – again"
or
Know the Rules and Guidelines

We used to have a columnist who drove me up the wall. Take note of the "used to have," which, being the bright, intuitive writer that you are, you know this particular writer was axed. Well, not literally, although I do admit the thought crossed my mind (refer back to "editor from hell... ").

This woman constantly brought in columns that contained segments of various copyrighted material, even though it was always edited out. The column was handwritten, very hard to read, usually much too long and had to be heavily edited because the grammar and spelling were atrocious. This particular author had been writing this "nostalgia-type" column for many years, but it soon became apparent that the paper was wasting a lot of time on the column, and on the writer, because she obviously thought the rules and guidelines did not apply to her. And since the day she was canned, we have not missed her or her column. We did have one subscriber who called in to say he missed her column. It was her husband. As an editor, I disqualified that complaint. I can do that, you know.

Later, we hired another writer to do the same type of column and she has been wonderful to work with. She knows what we want and she complies.

As a writer, make sure you are not high maintenance, or you will be replaced, usually very quickly. Know the paper's guidelines and try to stick to them as much as possible. Unless you're Ann Landers or Abigail VanBuren, you CAN be replaced.

What to Write?

Following are some examples of columns and features many weekly newspapers run on a somewhat regular basis:

Nostalgia-type column

This is usually written by a senior citizen. It should include tidbits of news from friends, family and the neighborhood, and mention community names, which, by the way, sells papers. Remembering the town's history, especially with accompanying photos, is always a good idea for this type of column.

Getting Published

Gardening tips/agriculture column
This should feature helpful tips and hints on gardening in that particular region.

Public figures soapbox
We used to have a superintendent at the local school who wrote a regular column as a way to communicate with the public on matters the school and school board were currently dealing with. This format can also be used for other public figures and/or organizations. Although they are typically written by the officials themselves, there's no reason why an experienced writer could not put together a series of columns featuring the public officials on a rotating basis.

Years ago column
This type of column can be researched at the local newspaper office or library. It's simply a compilation of facts that happened 5, 10, 25, 50 and even 100 years ago (if you're lucky enough to find some really old papers). The author of ours usually puts the front-page headlines, high school sports news (again, lots of names), births, and any other interesting events that grab her attention.

Child care center, nursery school, elementary, middle school, and high school news, etc.
These columns are great for two reasons. First of all, the facility gets some free publicity, and secondly, the public is kept informed on what is going on in their child's school or classroom environment.

This is also an excellent opportunity for any elementary or high school student who enjoys writing to gain experience and, at the same time, explore the world of journalism as a career option.

Slice of life columns
These are usually current, "chatty" columns detailing what's going on and what has recently happened in the area. Almost every paper I know has such a column. The ones that seem to be

the most popular have interesting anecdotes about local people and local happenings.

Movie review, restaurant review, or book review column

Some papers like to run this type of column and some don't. In our case, we might run the column if it is written by someone local. Local is almost always preferable. We've even been known to choose a column that is not quite as good or well-written over a better column, simply because the person writing it is a local resident.

We probably wouldn't consider a restaurant review column, simply because in this locale, there would only be a select few restaurants to review. Our sister paper does run a movie review column, written by a father and daughter team who live in that area, and we, at one time, also ran such a column.

Other Avenues

One way to get published in a weekly newspaper is to let them know you're available to freelance articles. Newspaper editors are always on the lookout for someone with quality writing skills who can step in and cover a school board, town council, or chamber of commerce story. And lest you think, "hmmm... that's just not the kind of writing I had in mind," remember this type of story is almost always front page news in a weekly paper.

And once you write a good town council story and have acquired the confidence of the editor and publisher, they will have no problem finding room for one of your feature stories.

To get started, write a feature story on a topic you think would be of interest to the newspaper's subscribers: a new business; the history of an old business; an interesting citizen (do you know someone who is 100 years old?); or maybe an interesting project the second graders over at Wekanreed Elementary are doing. There are thousands of stories in every community, waiting to be told, so just look around.

Getting Published

If you have any type of sports knowledge, most editors are, at some time or another, in need of a sports writer to cover local (usually high school) sports. If you have a child participating in sports, offer to cover the events for the local paper. Since you are a writer (you *are* a writer?) and must attend the events anyway, you might as well get paid for it. The editor will usually give you a camera and film and you can monopdize the paper with shots of your kid's stunning 3-pointers. On second thought, better take some of the *other* kids' pictures just to make it look good.

This might be a good time to point out that your stories should be *unbiased*. The newspaper's job is to report the facts, and let the public draw their own conclusions. Unless you're writing an editorial, do not editorialize.

Compile your story, with photos if you have them, and make an appointment to see the editor. Show them your story, tell them why it would be of interest to their readers, and then – here's the killer – offer to let them run it at no charge. Trust me, if they like the free article, then you can negotiate a price for future articles.

And Speaking of Money...

I think the best way to start this section is to be right up front and say – the MAIN advantage you should be looking for in getting published in a weekly newspaper is EXPOSURE, not MONEY.

If you're going in looking for big bucks, well, you need to turn to another chapter. Suffice it to say that most small newspapers sell for less than $20 a *year* per subscription. Which is why you sometimes see editors delivering pizza late at night, but don't get me started.

I called around and found that our rates are average compared to other weekly papers in our state. For a column or regular feature item, the going rate seems to be $5-$15 per piece. We pay $7 per column, unless it is a student writing a school news column, then the rate is $5 per column.

NEWSPAPERS

For freelance work, including feature articles, sports and business stories, etc., publishers pay about $10-$30 per article. We furnish our freelance reporters with cameras and film and pay $20 per story, which includes the photos.

For a feature photograph, most weekly papers pay $3-$5. I can't remember ever buying a photo, so you may not want to plan on feeding your family of four on what you will earn selling a weekly column or an occasional photograph.

The bottom line is, if you can write, you can get some excellent exposure in a weekly paper, not to mention that working with a deadline is also great discipline.

So, get your ideas down on paper, write an article or two, and go see that "editor from hell." Remember, all editors are writers, and if you can make their job a little easier, or add something of local interest to the paper, or increase the paper's readership, you'll have no problem getting published.

Oh yeah, and that "kissing up" thing won't hurt either.

NEWSPAPERS

IF YOU WANT TO WRITE ABOUT ENTERTAINMENT... READ THIS (AND THEN DECIDE!)
by Linda Cook

I've been writing for the *Quad-City Times* in Davenport, Iowa, for over a decade. Everybody, but everybody, wants my job writing features and entertainment news. But, although most of the time it's a lot of fun, it's not always easy.

The *Times* has a circulation of 57,000 – give or take – weekly, and more than 80,000 on Sunday. We cover the Quad-City region on both sides of the Mississippi River as well as the area that surrounds it.

I was hired at the *Times* as a clerk/inputter. That was after I worked several years as assistant editor at my hometown newspaper, *The Review Atlas*, also a daily. I graduated (never mind when) from Monmouth College with a Bachelor's Degree in elementary education/English. Although I did classroom work for three years during my college days, I never taught. I needed a job, period, right after college, so I took a job as a full-time proof reader and typesetter. I ran a now antiquated machine that, with each key punch on the regular keyboard, punched out a code on a paper tape. The tape was then run through a machine that translated the type with a laser, and printed out the finished product to be pasted up.

After I learned that now-outdated skill, I eventually began to write up obituaries and the society news about weddings, anniversaries and engagements, and I did an occasional feature story. Entertainment news and oddball feature stories were always my favorites. My first brush with fame was during a brief press conference when the late actor Burl Ives came to visit nearby Galesburg, Illinois. I never said a word because I was too awestruck; afraid to utter what might seem idiotic to this great man.

Getting Published

During the early 80's, Monmouth had a hot nightclub where, once in a while, stars such as The Grass Roots came for live performances. I met them – I remember that the leader (he still leads the band), Rob Grill, was especially kind to me. And that's also where I met Peter Tork of The Monkees fame.

Literally, I was a small-town girl who was decidedly unsure of herself around celebrities. Gradually, I overcame my shyness to ask a few simple questions or to do an occasional review, as I did when Herman's Hermits and The Ramones came to Galesburg. Gradually I began to do more hard news reporting, and I covered meetings, meetings, meetings from city councils to school boards to county boards. I learned how to converse with police chiefs and angry farmers, proud parents and mayors who had just lost an election.

A small paper isn't a good way to get started. It's an **excellent** way to get started, and here's why:

- If you're working for a weekly, your deadlines aren't as restrictive and you can add elements to the story after meetings or breaking news long after a daily reporter has reached deadline.
- You will be exposed to just about every conceivable kind of story and subject, from the town madman who writes regular rants to the paper to the kindly town philanthropist to homicides. You'll learn to talk to anyone about anything, and you'll learn in short order not to be, at least outwardly, judgmental, because the folks who were involved in that bar fight, the proprietors of that adult book store, and the new pastor at the Baptist Church will all know you, read what you write, and be happy to cancel their subscriptions if they don't think they've been treated fairly.
- You will learn diplomacy, especially if you cover city council meetings or any other kind of public body. Various sides on different issues will try to woo you to that particular side in hopes of swaying what you or an editorial writer might print. You'll be a well-balanced fence straddler if you stay open-minded.

NEWSPAPERS

- You will learn to handle a 35mm camera in any situation. Or, at least you should. You're writing the story, so you know best what kind of pictures you need. And this will make you doubly valuable in an industry that continues to downsize.
- You will also learn to watch what you say and do in your free time. Like it or not, everybody knows everybody else's business in a small town. And, like it or not, what you say and do reflects upon the integrity of your newspaper.

I worked for *The Atlas* for several years and took the job at the *Quad-City Times* in 1985. True, assignment-wise, it was several steps down the rung. But I wanted to work at a larger paper and – get this – the *Times* would pay me, for the first time in my life, a salary of five figures annually.

I thought I was rich, and I thought I was good enough to eventually be promoted all the way up the newsroom ladder. And here's where the going got really, really tough, because no one wanted to hear creative ideas from a clerk who was supposed to be inputting copy into the computer system. No one cared that I was a star back home. They just wanted good, clean copy.

I became an obituary reporter after just a few weeks. The night job, with Thursday and Friday off, was demanding. And that's where I learned to be fast and efficient, because a slip of the finger here or there could mean being written up and being put on probationary status the next day. I typed up business briefs, lengthy lists of award winners, obits, and copy from a variety of departments. And, because I made several typos during a month's time, it became clear to me that I needed to work extra hard to avoid any mistakes at all costs.

I began to take work home at night to proofread it. A month went by with no mistakes, and eventually several months and then a year. By then I began to seek a job as an entry level police reporter by applying for various jobs that opened. As I watched young people just out of journalism school being hired instead of

Getting Published

me, I began to realize that being timid and making no waves was not the way to get ahead.

So I became aggressive, even angry, in my requests to be promoted. And – eureka! – I was covering a potpourri of beats from religion to Bettendorf schools to obituaries. I filled in on city council meetings, county board meetings and committee meetings of all kinds, and the lay of the land was familiar because of my experience in Monmouth.

When I became the night cops reporter, I was in heaven, because I had always been interested in crime. Through that beat, I got to know coroners, police officers and hospital workers. Meanwhile, I asked an editor if I could do movie reviews after the movie reviewer, who had taken classes in cinema, quit to go to a different newspaper. I wrote one review, then another, and that was nine years and more than 1,700 movies ago.

In the meantime, I was promoted to the features department, where my boss really encouraged creativity and flexibility. Now I'm responsible for stories about upcoming events in our "GO!" magazine, which is all about entertainment; our "Weekend" section that runs on Saturday; news about exhibits at local museums and art galleries as well as local artists. Also I write day-trip travel stories, personality profiles and concert reviews, interview various performers coming to the area, and write breaking news about arts and leisure, from a museum's purchase of a new Grant Wood painting to the local filming of a movie.

This sounds corny, I know, but I love my job. Here are a few tips that would have made my life easier if I had followed them 11 years ago:

• Know your "kid glove" sources and readers who, for one reason or another, must be handled with same. Ask questions of your fellow reporters, who will help you run the gamut of callers and drop-ins, from chronic complainers and potentially dangerous individuals to whistle blowers.

NEWSPAPERS

- This one is simple, but it's difficult to follow: Be nice on the phone. Yes, the woman on the other end of the line has difficulty hearing you, and doesn't understand that you didn't write the story about the Little League team that includes her nephew. But part of your job is being patient, and helping her get through to an honest-to-goodness human voice who can answer her questions or deal with her complaints.
- This one is even more simple and even more difficult: Follow through. Don't blow people off, and don't lie. If a caller wants to know what's happening May 15, don't tell him you'll get back to him and then not return his call or request. Don't promise a story that you'll never deliver, under any circumstances. It makes you look bad. It makes the entire paper look bad.
- Know where to find information that might help callers. Begin by having access – Rolodex or telephone directory – of numbers such as the local theaters, stages, tourism bureaus and information desks at local libraries. People call newspapers not just to report news but also to find out news that's important to them. You don't have to know when the McDonald's Collectors Convention will be held in Oak Brook, but it's nice to have access to someone with that information for a caller.
- Enjoy talking on the phone. I average 10-20 calls daily, along with people arriving at my desk to drop off press releases. Of course, you need not feel obligated to baby-sit folks with too much time on their hands, but you do need to politely tell them when it's time for you to hang up.

For Entertainment Writers Only

Expect to be bombarded with press releases and phone calls asking for your "help" to sell tickets (this translates as "free publicity"). You need to look for different angles to present the information more than once to keep it fresh. Have you already written about a local play that's being performed? Then interview the playwright about what inspired him and turn that into a personality profile.

Getting Published

Can't get an interview with the rock star who's coming to town? Then talk to someone behind the scenes at the auditorium for a story about the performer's demands – did he want filet mignon or just an endless supply of Milky Way bars? How many trucks of equipment is he bringing? What does his light show involve? And how about a review of the singer's most recent CD?

If you manage to get an interview – good for you – then you'll probably get only 10-15 minutes on the phone with the performer. Keep in mind, this person probably will be doing phoners all day long, which means she may not be in the best mood, and may be tired of hearing, "What's your favorite number to perform?" Start with the person's childhood (and that doesn't go just for performers, either), because that's when, almost always, the seed of performing was planted. Did she come from a musical family? Did her mother force her to take piano lessons when she really wanted to play the harp?

Be familiar with the music of the performer, even if it's only the song titles. The more you know about the person's music, the more questions you can ask and the better an interview will be.

Local performers are only too happy to talk about their music, and they'll probably shower you with CDs and offers of free tickets. Find out your company policy about accepting freebies before you take anything that could be considered a bribe.

For Reviewers Only

Develop your own set of standards for reviews – from restaurants to CD-ROM games to concerts – and stick to them.

Remember that a review is only an opinion, and every single one of your readers has the right to disagree with you (and sometimes it may seem that they simultaneously do). If someone writes a letter to the editor about your hideous, unfair review, take heart and remember that the letter is slamming your review and not you personally. If you get many angry calls and letters, especially about a particular review, re-examine your standards. Were you

NEWSPAPERS

too harsh? Did you let your traffic ticket earlier that day cloud what you wrote?

Remember that local theatre troupes aren't professionals. They work hard, long hours to be on that stage, and they deserve a second chance and/or the benefit of doubt.

If you write a column, people will recognize you from your photo. Acknowledge people kindly when they recognize you, even if they say something like, "Gee, you don't look that fat in the paper." You don't have to answer every question, though. Your salary, your politics and your religious beliefs don't need to be the center of brief conversation with a stranger.

Don't take yourself, or uncalled for criticism, too seriously.

SELF-PUBLISHING
by Jana Lynn Shellman

You have to be very, very brave or very naïve, or both to make the decision to self-publish without a great deal of thought. When I decided to self-publish *The Wish Factory: How to Make Wishes Come True*, I thought I was doing it to solve a problem. Publishers, being very busy people, wouldn't look at it long enough or in enough detail to understand the meaning of it, or to understand the reason for it. It seemed a simple matter to bypass the publishers by doing it myself; because I, being the book's mother, believe it to be second only in importance to my son, who is the most wonderful being in the world. I'm sure you feel exactly the same way about your writing product as I felt about *The Wish Factory*. My mother told me long ago, "Never say, My child is perfect." So it was not until many people told me, "You have a terrific kid," that I believed this was not just a mother's prejudice. The same was true of the book... it was only after a lot of people told me, "*The Wish Factory* is a terrific book," that I began to believe it was not only my author's prejudice. Luckily, I do possess the ability to stand back and look at a project and detach myself emotionally from it. I did this with *The Wish Factory* and evaluated whether or not I should self-publish it.

I was encouraged by several things. Friends kept pointing out many Number One Bestsellers were originally self-published, including *The Celestine Prophecy* by James Redfield. I learned Benjamin Franklin, Samuel Clemens, Zane Grey, Louise Hay and Peter McWilliams were also self-publishers. This gave me hope. Before I went very far into the project, I examined my reasons for wanting to see the book published. I made a list.

Why I Want To See My Book Published
1. The book has an important message to help people find happiness, prosperity, and control in their lives.

Getting Published

    2.   I'm tired of running off computer copies and giving them away.

    3.   I've tried hard for four years to get it published the "normal" way, having submitted it to hundreds of publishers, and I want to get on to other projects.

Number 3 above is a fallacy. I wanted to stop marketing and get on with writing. I'm lucky to get 30 minutes a day to write!

I must admit it hadn't occurred to me I would get great pleasure from seeing my name in print, but I do. I think it's incredibly good for the ego, and we should all take very good care of our own ego. There are all too many who will step in to do otherwise.

In beginning my study of self-publishing, I read a year's worth of *Publishers' Weekly*; a year's worth of *Small Press Magazine*, a book called *The Complete Guide to Self-Publishing,* written by Tom & Marilyn Ross and published by their publishing company, About Books, Inc. and another book called *Book Blitz,* about book promotion.

I telephoned several major publishers and asked them these questions:

    1.   How much money would you invest in an unknown author's non-fiction book?

    2.   How much would you pay for promotion and publicity?

    3.   How many books would you order?

I was surprised by the answers. They were almost the same for three of the largest publishers. They don't invest relatively much at all, and the budget for promotion and publicity is very small. The number of books printed depended upon many things but was normally small for a new author.

I learned more about publisher's promotion and publicity of books in October of 1994, when I attended Magna Cum Murder at Muncie, Indiana. It was a gathering of mystery fans and mystery authors. I attended because I'm also a mystery writer and wanted to mingle. I met many authors and was terribly impressed by the promotional tours they make each year, the low budget for them, and how much of their own money they spend promoting their own books. It seemed to me unless you were a blockbuster author, you weren't about to get much publicity assistance from your publisher.

SELF-PUBLISHING

I reasoned as a self-publisher, I wouldn't have to pay myself an advance, and I could take the amount a big publisher would pay for an advance and apply it toward promotion and publicity.

Finally, I was facing an uncertain future with my employer. I took out a loan in November, using my car for collateral, reasoning it more practical to obtain a loan while I still had a job than to wait and have full title to a car but no way to borrow on it. I came home with $10,000. I also applied for a couple of extra credit cards and began negotiating to sell my share of some rental properties.

As a practical matter, I examined my financial situation, and with my experience as a bankruptcy paralegal, decided sink or swim, I would not lose my house or my car. If you are going to borrow money to start a self-publishing project, or any business, taking out a second mortgage is not a bad idea because should you fail, bankruptcy law allows you to exempt only up to $7,500 in equity in your house for an individual and $15,000 for a couple. If you have any equity over that you might be forced to sell your house to pay of f your debts. You can exempt $1,500 equity in your car. This may seem a very pessimistic way to plan ahead, unless you know me well. I was also planning how to spend my multiple-millions in sales, and I had my new house designed and laid out!

The law office was closed from the week before Christmas until two weeks after New Year's. I took that time to begin my self-publishing adventure. I determined I wanted to produce a product that could stand beside other professionally produced books. I didn't want it to look homemade.

Advance Book Information and ISBN Numbers

A year prior to the professional production of my book, I printed 100 copies of a shorter version that I gave away for Christmas or sold to a few people for $5 each. I tried to peddle a few of them to local bookstores, but they didn't want them because they didn't have ISBN numbers or bar codes. It was also pointed out to me the book's 8 ½ "x 11" size was awkward for most bookstore shelves.

Getting Published

To obtain ISBN numbers write to R.R. Bowker, 121 Chanlon Road, New Providence, NJ 07974, or call them at (908) 665-6770. They will send you an "Application for an ISBN Publisher Prefix." There is a one-time charge of $115 and they will send you ten numbers. You must put these numbers in a safe place, because it costs more to have the company look them up.

When they send you your numbers, they will also send you a supply of Advance Book Information sheets. This sheet is very important because it lists your book in their publications, "Forthcoming Books" and "Books in Print." The information also goes on their CDs and computer data bases, and it is the information used by all other distributors for their data bases.

Library of Congress Number

The Library of Congress catalog card number is printed on your copyright page. Over 20,000 libraries use this system for ordering books. If you want libraries to order your books, you must have a Library of Congress number. Write for a 'Request for Preassignment of LCCN Number,"Washington, D.C. 20559, or call (202) 707-3000.

EAN BOOKLAND Scanning Symbol

Most bookstores will refuse to carry your book if it does not have an EAN BOOKLAND Scanning Symbol. This symbol carries much of the information about the book, including the price. It is the method bookstores use for ordering the book, inventory, and sales. This is probably second in importance to the ISBN number. It costs far less. The scanning symbol for *THE WISH FACTORY* cost $12.

You should tell the supplier the size of the space you wish to fill. You need to ask your printer whether he wants positive or negative film, and whether he wants 'tight reading with emulsion up or emulsion down." They need to know whether you want the OCR-A/ISBN above or below the EAN bar-code symbol. If you dont tell them they do it the way most other publishers request it. You should ask for 92% magnification as well as bar width reduction (BWR) of .001. You must include the price of

SELF-PUBLISHING

your book and your book's ABN number. You're going to learn all sorts of things like this that you never wanted to know.

There are many suppliers of the bar code. I faxed all of the information to FOTEL (708) 834-5250. You can write to them at FOTEL, 41 West Home Avenue, Villa Park, IL 60181. I received my negative in two days.

Binding

You must decide what sort of bindings your book is going to have. I chose "perfect binding" and a trade paperback size because it is the most practical in terms of costs. I researched bookstores and decided my book would fit on the shelf with other inspirational how-to books. Most of them were 8½" x 5½" and were either hardcover or trade paperbacks. Plus retailers like binding that have the title of the book on the spine. They take up less space.

Cover

While I was looking at books in the stores I made note of the way clerks placed them on the shelf and the colors that drew my attention. White covers with red titles and mustard yellow covers with red titles were the first books I noticed, but the mustard yellow didn't please my eye as much. I felt the most appealing books had blue and/or hot pink on them, as well. I put all of these colors on my cover, with a red title on a white background for the spine.

I kept hiring artists to do the cover art for me, and no one could produce the cover I saw in my mind. My mother pointed out I'd been to art school and was somewhat of an artist myself, so I finally did the artwork on the cover. I designed a cover with a white background, red title, a mustard yellow sub-title with a blue teddy bear and a hot pink angel.

I used a Sharpie fine point to draw the outlines of my work on transparency plastics and used acrylics to paint the characters. I printed out my titles and all other print on transparencies on a laser printer. Everything was cut out and moved around until it was just right. I taped these transparency pieces to an art board.

Getting Published

As well as allowing 8½" x 5½" for the front and for the back, you must allow the width of the spine, so you need to know just how many "sigs" your book will have. "Sigs" are signatures: 32-page groups that the book will be printed in. I printed out the book exactly as it would look when sent to the printer, then did back-to-back sets in sigs. This gave me a close idea of the thickness of the book. You measure your book width, back and front, plus the spine. I took my finished layouts to a lithography company specializing in four-color process, and had them do the four-color separations. Although everything was printed on the laser printer in black, the lithographer will help you sort through colors, and choose all of the colors for the titles and for each object on the cover.

The approximate cost of this process was $800 for the four-color separations. I chose a four-color cover over a cheaper one- or two-color cover, because the larger printers charge approximately the same amount for all covers regardless of the number of colors, and I reasoned the cover would have more appeal in four colors. I believe it was worth the extra $800 for the separations. Bookstore clerks tell me customers pick up the book, turn it over, and often buy it without looking inside.

Title

If your muse chooses your title, you don't have much choice but to go with it. That's what happened with *The Wish Factory*. But I did come up with the sub-title, *How to Make Wishes Come true*. I chose the sub-title for two reasons: To describe the contents of the book, and to titillate the customer's sense of curiosity. Seeing my title in print has given me far more satisfaction than seeing my name on the cover. It's somewhat like seeing your child's name in the paper for being on the honor roll.

Designing the Book

The simplest way to design your book is to look at hundreds of popular books and just do it the same way. You'll note there's almost always a blank page, then a title page with nothing but the title, there's

SELF-PUBLISHING

a blank page on the back of that, then another title page showing the author and publisher as well. Backing that page is the "copyright" page, showing your publishing information, your copyright statement, your ISBN number, your LCCN number, and much more. Examine the copyright page in *The Complete Guide to Self-Publishing*. They've got it all there.

Following the copyright page can be your Dedication Page, Acknowledgments Page, Foreword, Introduction, the body of your book, and the Bibliography, the Afterword, and sometimes a "meet the author" page. You can fill in with more blank pages if you want full sigs.

Content determines the size of your book, but you should try to design your book so it fits in multiples of full sigs. This is the least expensive way to print the book. It is less expensive to have four sigs, which include empty, unprinted pages, than it is to have 3½ sigs.

I did several mock-ups of the book design, using computer printouts. I laid out the book using WordPerfect 6.0 with By Design, and some pages were designed using Microsoft Publisher. It helped to have a scanner, and if I were doing it again, I'd have a full-page scanner.

Printers

I telephoned several small printers in the area. The prices were not happy ones. I called back the publishers I'd talked to before, and learned the price of paper was up and the prices they'd quoted to me six months earlier were no longer good. While I was at it, I asked for the names of the printers they hired to do their work. (By the way, they don't call it "printing"... they call it "book manufacturing"). You can get a book at the library called *Directory of Book Printers*. I also found a magazine with an article naming the top three printers. I contacted them by letter, and then by phone, and obtained a quantity price.

The printers' price quotes I received were all very much alike and were for 3,000 copies, with a quote for each additional thousand, as well as a quote for additional covers. While I was asking, I asked

Getting Published

them to give me a time line from the time they receive the copy until I would receive the printed books on my doorstep. This time line varies according to the time of year you place your order, a fact you should keep in mind for reruns. Mid to late summer is a bad time to order books printed, due to the high demand for school book printing, as well as for printing for Christmas orders. Right after Christmas is the best and shortest time to order books and get quick delivery.

I chose one of the country's largest printers because it did not appear to me the price varied much, and I reasoned they would be the most experienced in book printing and would provide me with the most professional appearance. I've examined products of other self-publishers who went with smaller printers, and I believe it was a good idea to trust the job to a more experienced book printer.

My first printing was for 5,000 books. The total cost was just a little less than $1 per book if you figure the cost of the preparation of the color separations for the four-color cover ($800), and the printing and shipping costs of the book, and the $200 I spent for the 2,000 additional covers. The printer discovered an error in the four-color separations and was able to make the necessary adjustments and changes in the plant. I believe I benefited greatly from their experience and professionalism.

I also print brochures, order forms, biographical sheets, press kits and the like. For these print jobs, I purchase the paper through a jobber and I have the printing done at a Co-op printer, who does the work for 20% of the cost union printers would charge for the same job. For instance, I just had 1,200 try-fold brochures printed and folded for $22. The requirements are to make at least $10 per year donation or to volunteer our time. I tack an extra $5 on to every print job. It is well worth it.

Extra Covers

While you are printing your book it doesn't hurt to have extra covers printed. I had 2,000 printed. I cut some of them in two and have postcards to mail out to bookstores and for other promotional occasions.

SELF-PUBLISHING

Distributors

I told you before, I thought I was self-publishing to solve a problem of not being able to interest the people who would publish it. I have, ultimately, solved that problem. There are now publishers paying attention and taking an interest, but in the long run, the problem was merely persistence. Perhaps if I'd been more persistent I would have attracted the proper publisher. Instead I traded a difficulty interesting a publisher for the difficulty of interesting distributors and bookstores. The answer to both of those problems was merely being persistent, refusing to take "No" for an answer, and learning not to take rejection personally. Nothing is impossible, and never, never, never, never give up. Remember my motto... no matter what goals you pursue... "It's always too soon to give up."

The most important thing to do to get nationwide coverage for your book is to list it with Baker & Taylor Co., P.O. Box 6920 (652 East Main Street), Bridgewater, NJ 08807. And once you've paid your money, check carefully to see they've got all of the information correct. Ultimately, a good four months of my time, and a chunk of my promotional money went for naught, because Baker & Taylor had my book listed as not published until August, when it was actually published in March. I was on numerous radio talk shows, did massive direct mailings, and even telephoned to push the book, and when anyone called a bookstore to order the book, they were told it wasn't available until August! I am in negotiation with Baker & Taylor to rectify this problem now.

The biggest difficulty with interesting distributors is getting it out to all of the major bookstores first. So if you have any pull at all with the major stores, I recommend you use it. The sooner you can get it into the major bookstores, the better off you will be. Getting it before the public takes a great deal of work.

Promotion and Publicity

This area is probably the most fun for me. As a result of my promotional advertising I've been on many radio and television talk

Getting Published

shows to promote the book. I am presently working on a lecture tour doing motivational talks. This will also allow me to sell copies of the book – for the retail price – at each of these speaking engagements.

One of the most important things to learn right away is you are the best promoter of your book, and you must learn right now to get rid of any stage fright you have or any hesitancy you have about public speaking, because, in order to promote your book, you're going to have to do a great deal of it. Even if you get someone else to publish it.

I advertised in a publication called *Radio-TV Interview Report* that goes to most radio and television show producers. As a result of my ads I've been on many radio and television talk shows plugging my book. As soon as I know I'm going to be broadcasting from an area, I call the public library and ask them to fax me the yellow pages for bookstores from the area. I do a mailing directed at the bookstores, which usually includes a copy of my cover which has excerpts from the book printed on the back. Other times I will send out a postcard made from the cover, which I've laser-printed on the back with information about the particular broadcast, urging bookstores to order books. This has worked nicely in most areas. It is my personal belief authors must put forth extraordinary effort in order to promote their book into the public spotlight.

Handling Rejection

Whether you're a self-publisher or trying to sell to a publisher, you have to learn to handle rejection of your work. Keep in mind, rejection slips are not necessarily a reflection of your writing ability. Some very famous authors have had their most prominent works rejected innumerable times. This did not detract from the value of their writing.

Just because Walker rejected your mystery novel is no reason not to send it back to them the next year and the next year and the year after that! Chances are the readers have all been shuffled at least a dozen times; chances are new editors have come and gone; and chances are, if a reader or an editor recognizes the name of your novel, they might just think "I've heard of this book" and they might just read it all! The same for every other publisher there is. Be persistent. If you get back a stock rejection slip, don't let it stop you from submitting your book again right away. If you get a personalized rejection with constructive criticism, read it carefully, study your work, and see if the criticism is justified. If it is, make the changes, and submit it back to the same editor once again. But never stop submitting your work. Remember, it's always too soon to give up.

Evaluating Your work for Self-publishing

Is your project non-fiction? If it is, it probably has more potential for self-publication than a work of fiction.

Is there a limited market for your work? If so, it is probably more practical for you to self-publish.

If you didn't sell one single copy, could you afford the money and the time spent on the project?

Do you have what it takes to handle self-promotion and publicity of the book? If you don't, you should probably opt for selling it to a publisher.

You must believe your book is important and of benefit to the greater good of society and that people will be better for its having existed. Foremost, your mind should be on your product's benefit to others rather than on the benefit of its sales. I believe your profits will equal demand, and you will have a successful product.

Remember, you are only limited by the number of obstacles your mind can manufacture!

THE BOOK DOCTOR: WHY I GET PAID TO DO WHAT I DO
by Matthew V. Clemens

Everyone, it is said, has at least one good book in them. I don't argue that. The problem is a lot of people go into writing without knowing anything about it. Having a book inside you does not mean that you have the ability to get it out. But let's assume, since you're reading this book, that you have not only a wonderful story but the skills to tell it.

If you're like most beginning writers, you've told your idea to your family and friends, and unless they don't like you, they say, "That's a really good idea, you should write the book."

So you do.

They – your friends and family – read the book and say, "That's really good, you should get that published."

This, my friend, is where the book doctor comes in.

Unless your friends and family are writers themselves, and for most of us that is a big NOT, they read like readers. Readers will tell you whether the story holds their interest and whether or not they like the hero and villain. That's important, but of more importance is the opinion of someone who reads like a writer. There's a difference. Reading like a writer involves looking past all the things that a pleasure reader is looking for.

Pleasure readers are looking to be transported to another place – to become so involved in the story that they forget that it's 1:00 a.m. and they have a 7:00 a.m. meeting and need to get some sleep. My job is to help the writer transport the reader.

The only way that happens is to get the book published in the first place. The last figure quoted to me by someone within the publishing industry was that 3,000 unsolicited manuscripts find their way to New York each week. It's not my intention to scare you away from this, but you can do the math as well as I can. There are only five or six major publishing houses left in New

Getting Published

York. Each has a staff of perhaps 10 readers. That's maybe 60 readers to wade through 3,000 manuscripts per week.

If you're going to be number 3,001, you want to have the best possible opportunity for the brief time your manuscript is going to be on an editor's desk.

Let's take a moment to talk about publishing. Publishing and writing are like apples and polar ice caps. They exist on the same planet but have very little else in common. The book that you have slaved over for a year, that is your heart and soul poured out on 400 pages, to an editor is a property, not even your property, just property. The editor that receives your book is looking equally for two things:

A. The next *Gone With the Wind*, and

B. A reason to put your book down and get to the next property. Bear in mind also that the editor may have a case of the flu, fought with his/her spouse before work, spilled coffee on his/her new suit, or been berated by the boss for falling behind. All these things will affect how this editor looks at your book.

Therefore, you want to increase your chances of being the next *Gone With the Wind* by presenting the best written, most professional looking manuscript that the editor will see. How do you do that when you've never written a book before nor ever sent anything to New York? You hire a book doctor who will do the things that your friends and family haven't.

If your friends do suggest changes to your book they will usually be what the reader wants to see, which is not necessarily what the book needs. A book doctor will look for things that will improve the book and still maintain the integrity of what the writer set forth originally.

For instance, does the writer use strong verbs, does the writer rely on adverbs, do the characters behave in a manner which is logical for that character, are there flaws in the logic of the plot? Don't laugh at this one. I know of one book, a James Bondian type adventure that was reasonably well written, in which the entire plot centered around a drug deal gone bad because of a Christmas Day snow storm in

BOOK DOCTOR

Buenos Aires. The problem? Christmas Day in Argentina is in the middle of summer.

The writer had written herself into a corner that she couldn't get out of. Since so much of the book was dependent on that storm, the entire manuscript ended up in a waste can because of it. A book doctor could have saved this woman embarrassment, and more importantly, possibly been able to salvage the manuscript by offering some suggestions on how to fix the problem.

Another writer that I work with wrote a political thriller in which a major female character, a CNN anchorperson, who through her ex-husband, the hero of the book, became aware of a plot to assassinate a major political figure. When she had fulfilled her purpose in the book, she simply disappeared. I mentioned to the author that a career woman in that field probably wouldn't just walk away from the story that would make her career.

He agreed, wrote the woman back into the end of the novel, and the book went on to sell half a million copies. Now even I'm not egocentric enough to think that was the reason the book sold so well. However, both the author and I felt that the extra input enhanced the final product.

There are literally hundreds of things that a book doctor will look for that will help to make the material more saleable. I'm just going to list some of the things that I take into account when I'm being paid to doctor a book, because if I were to go into all of them in detail this section alone would be 300 pages. As I've mentioned, I look for plot logic, strong verbs, specific wording, and fully developed characters. Plus, I check for realistic dialogue and characters that have distinct voices. Other considerations include the tone, clarity, pace, word order, sentence order, and repetitiveness. I suggest alternatives intended to heighten suspense or make a character more believable. I stroke egos, conjugate verbs and dangle participles when necessary.

Good writers are nice, but great storytellers make more money. My job is to help you become the best storyteller possible. The purpose of a book doctor is exactly the same as the purpose of this book – to help you get published.

BIOGRAPHY

REASSEMBLING THE DUST
By Wes D. Gehring

In writing a number of biographies, I have found there is an ever-increasing interest in the genre. At its most basic it is history made personal; it is a side door into another era.

Biographies are also popular because no matter how famous the subject, the reading audience shares many basic rite of passage experiences with the figure, from child rearing to how they were reared as children. This shared human condition represents finding the universal in the particular. Readers of my own biographies often initially noted how much they had in common with the subject.

It takes me one to two years to research and write a biography. I am assisted time-wise because many of my subjects, including Charlie Chaplin, W.C. Fields, Laurel & Hardy, the Marx Brothers, and Robert Benchley, were comedy contemporaries. Thus, I have more than a head start on the period.

When you pick a subject to chronicle, you need to have a great interest in the person as you will be spending the better part of the next two or three years with the individual. The subject will become part of your family. Indeed, family members might claim the subject has become the dominant member of the household!

Luckily, my dad and both grandfathers all loved comic performers and playing the humorist. There was no question that all things funny took precedence over everything else. While this occasionally had less than positive repercussions for me a la the trials of being a class clown, it enabled me to point toward my current biography research at an early age. That is, while comedy performers were forever celebrated in my family, there was no analytical discussion of the artists and how their careers came about and I developed a keen curiosity about this aspect of the performers' lives. Consequently, I knew well before college that I wanted to chronicle the lives of American film comedians.

Getting Published

The fascination with a clown's background has always sustained society. Clowns comically comfort us in our short lives with their resilience – both physical and spiritual. Along the same lines, society seems most fascinated with the clown biography that reveals tragic roots – the ability to provoke laughter despite personal sadness. For instance, in my biography of Robert Benchley, I examined the chilling statement inadvertently uttered by his mother in the eight-year old's presence upon the death of a beloved older brother, "Oh, why couldn't it have been Robert?"

Consequently, Benchley's later comedy success, despite his mother's numbing plea when her favorite son died, is the stuff of comic legend – humor's version of the phoenix. And a goldmine for the biographer. Moreover, the plea and Benchley's early lack of maternal attention has more recently shown that elementary age children with a marked sense of humor are more likely to have had a lack of early motherly attention.

While there are no hard and fast rules for the comedian biography, the previous statement certainly applies to my most highly visible writing – on Groucho Marx. In a recent *A & E Biography* segment on the comedian, I joined with the Marx family and friends in discussing his mother's preference for older brothers Chico and Harpo. The accepted assumption was that this third-class status undoubtedly contributed both to Groucho's drive to succeed (to impress this woman so taken with show business) and to the often misogynous nature of his comedy.

Cinema's most celebrated comedic figure and the subject of my first biography was Charlie Chaplin. But he did not suffer from the lack of a mother's love. However, his early years were like a Dickens tragedy, with his single-parent mother fighting poverty and a descent into madness. Thus, once again the biographer finds the resilience which can create laughter regardless of pain.

My fascination with Chaplin was fed by the encouragement of my biography loving maternal grandfather, whose own Irish immigrant father had been captivated by this transplanted English

BIOGRAPHY

clown with the east-west feet. Consequently, as a child, I collected Chaplin super-8 movie short subjects and read everything I could find on him. My first serious biographical writing would address "Charlie," or as the comedian labeled him, "the little fellow."

My interest in comedy is a perfect match for my absorption with biography, which author Paul Mariani has described, with dark comedy, as "reassembling the dust." It is an introspective time, as the biographer is made to more closely consider his own life.

This writing genre plays upon a phenomenon known as "angles of vision." This metaphor is especially rich because it addresses both the specific attitudes any incoming biographer might have about the subject and the changing "angles of vision." The same author will undergo change as he or she spends years with the subject. Indeed, the connection can become so strong the biographer sometimes finds himself rooting for a subject to take a different path, despite obviously already knowing the individual's story.

"Angles of vision" represents the rich new perspective each successive biographer brings to a given subject – the ready defense of the multi-profiled life of any unique personality. Each reevaluation brings one closer to that comic observation so pertinent to the biographer's art: "There are two reasons why a man does anything. There's a good reason and there's the real reason."

The "angle of vision" perspective can also be applied to your subject. How did his outlook vary through the years? How did it mesh with a different era's status quo? For instance, the screen image of Stan Laurel is that of an asexual antihero. Yet in real life he was a much-married ladies' man. And he observed of his many wedding ceremonies: "It's one way of throwing a party."

In recent years there has been a tendency for the biographer himself to surface briefly in the work. Orson Welles encouraged his last biographer to do this when examining the conflicting views of Welles she encountered when interviewing people for her book.

Getting Published

This suggestion is strikingly reminiscent of the reporter in Welles' classic film *Citizen Kane* (1941), who is trying to track down the meaning of "Rosebud," the title character's last words.

In my Marx Brothers biography I found reason for a personal reference. I was doing research at an archive some distance from my home. On different nights I treated myself to two then-current commercial theater releases: Woody Allen's *Hannah and Her Sisters* (1986) and Terry Gilliam's *Brazil* (1985). Though both are comedies in the broadest sense of the word, they are radically different. Allen's work is personality comedy which ends with hope; Gilliam's film is darkest comedy – a slapstick *1984*. Both of these very different celebrated films used Marx Brothers clips as cultural symbols of equally varied things. Here, there was a Marx Brothers researcher who tried – and failed – on two successive nights, to find a simple, momentary escape from his focus of study. That failure would seem to say a lot about the ongoing significance of the Marxes, especially since *Hannah and Her Sisters* and *Brazil* have known great critical acclaim.

The biographer must also watch for information in omissions. In Chaplin's lengthy autobiography there is no mention in the text of Stan Laurel. Yet they were vaudeville roommates in their touring years. Chaplin was a unique talent, but such a deletion supports the view that his vanity kept him from acknowledging people who might have had some influence on him.

A pivotal challenge to the biographer is eventually moving beyond the research. You have to realize that despite the mounds of books and papers around your desk, you can never find all the facts. A biographer's goal should be to find the "best truth," which is better than invention. Conversely, an untruth sometimes can be helpful. For example, for decades there has been an ongoing debate among baseball fans as to whether Babe Ruth actually "called" a homerun blast in the early 1930's. The truth here is not so important as the phenomenon that people want to believe he was capable of doing anything.

BIOGRAPHY

Frequently, visiting the home or the surroundings of his subject's youth can assist the biographer. In doing a biography of Laurel & Hardy, my stay in Laurel's Ulverston, England was very helpful. Most importantly it explained his great love of the sea which rivaled that of comedy. From the hills around the village, where children still play, is a breathtaking view of the Irish Sea. And his birthplace is still intact, as is the grocery where he bought candies. It was like examining a piece of time – Stan Laurel's time.

Smelling salts can also be helpful during research. I worked closely with the Benchley family on his biography. And at one point I noted that several of his adult diaries were missing. I was calmly told that they had been burned because they were not flattering to the humorist. I nearly had a heart attack, but I kept my composure. The family had been very helpful and I did not want to risk all that by yelling, "You did what?" I even recited the story about President Truman requesting to see the love letters he had written his wife. She simply said, "I burned them." Shocked, Truman said, "But think of history!" And she replied, "I was."

George Orwell once suggested that all writing is essentially an act of ego – the audacity that you have something important to say. While I would never deny this, the rest of the story (at least for me) is about self-discovery, from why I find some comedians so funny, to how writing a biography is a very personalized look at both history ... and yourself.

Getting Published

THE SUBMISSION PACKAGE

All right, you've heard *what* the pros have to say about their genre. Now let's talk about the *how*, as in how you get your writing in front of the editor.

It's a fact; properly submitting your work is the point at which many aspiring authors fall apart. The same bravado, conviction, and confidence that enabled you to plow your way through three or four hundred pages are required again. Your painstaking hours of editing and all those agonizing decisions you made searching for just the right word or phrase are all on the line. The word turning, the gut wrenching, the dictionary searching, the lonely hours – all come down to this. It's called *selling* your book.

So, how do you do this?

You have some *professional* read it. When I say *professional*, I'm not talking about your mother who thinks every word you write borders on sheer brilliance. Nor am I talking about your significant other just because 'they read a lot." Nor am I talking about members of your writer's support group (unless, of course, they are all published authors and are more than passingly familiar with your genre). No, now you have to share your work with true professionals.

For some reason, a large percentage of writers I know pale at the thought of putting a submission package together. I admit I choked the first time I submitted a novel. The fact that I had spent the better part of my adult life in corporate marketing didn't help a bit. It was easy to sell my company's product. Rejections didn't hurt because I knew they weren't personal; after all, I didn't make the product, I only marketed it.

Selling your writing is a different matter. It's your soul, your sweat, and your hope for the future that are on the line. What if – heaven forbid – they don't like it?

Let's get past that trying, chafing, irksome, distressing thought here and now. Raise your right hand and solemnly repeat after me:

SUBMISSION

"I, _____ , am going to put together the most professional submission package humanly possible."

That wasn't so hard, was it?

Now, let's do it. And to do it, you need to construct the three key elements of the submission package: the query letter, the writer's resume (including your press clippings) and the synopsis of your novel or the proposal if your work is non-fiction.

The Query Letter

Think of it this way: a query letter is your business card.
- A query letter is your introduction to an editor or agent.
- A query letter is the first impression you make on the professionals who are going to evaluate your writing efforts.

Remember what they say about first impressions? Keep in mind that the impression you want to create for that editor or agent who has just opened that submission package is that you are a professional.

To start with, a query letter should be one page. It should be meticulously typed and flawless in every respect. Keep this in mind; the purpose of your letter is to pique the interest of some of the world's most skeptical and picky people.

A query letter should be concise. It should contain a very brief synopsis of your manuscript. (I've had more than one editor tell me that if a writer can't reduce the essence of their work down to 25 words – they really haven't nailed that manuscript down to its most tightly written fashion.)

A query letter should be written in a no-nonsense business format.

A query letter should be addressed to a specific agent or a specific editor at a particular publisher.

A query letter should contain an opening sentence that is both a hook and a statement of purpose.

A query letter should contain that very brief synopsis or proposal statement (average length 25 words) that we discussed earlier.

Getting Published

A query letter should state that your manuscript is complete and available.

Got all that? Okay – some of you are probably thinking all of the above isn't going to fit on one page. Wrong, you can do it. Some of you are thinking you can't reduce your 400-page manuscript to a brief 25-word synopsis. Wrong again, you can do that too. Granted, it does take a little practice.

Now that you know what the essence of a good query letter is, let's go into it in more detail.

Let's start with the no nonsense format. If you are the least bit uncertain about what constitutes the format of a good business letter, don't guess. Every basic communication textbook contains a section on the appropriate style for formal or business correspondence. If you don't have one handy and your local library is fifty miles of rocky road away, call a friend who is a top-flight secretary and have them tell you what goes where. If all else fails, we have included an example of business letter format in this section.

Please understand, a well-written, professional business letter won't sell your book. But one that is poorly written can kill any chances you may have had of making a sale. All a well-written professional query letter will accomplish is to entice the editor or agent to read your entire letter – and perhaps move on to other parts of your submission package. Look at it this way – if you can't write a well-written query letter, why should the editor or agent assume that your manuscript would be written any better?

It should go without saying, but I'll say it anyway. Use good stationery: Substantial weight, white bond, and of course, personalized stationery is best. Obviously, you do not use stationery that has little kitty cats up in the corner, is some color other than white, or is perfumed. You want them to regard you as a professional – remember?

Another important point: Always address your submission package to a specific person. Double-check the editor's or agent's name and be certain of the correct spelling. Is it Mr., Ms., or Mrs.? Double-check the agency's or publisher's name, along with the address, and make certain the spelling is correct. If you don't know, invest in a phone call, double-check your source of information and make sure it's correct.

Date your letter. If somewhere down the road it becomes necessary to call the agent or editor, you'll come across as a great deal more professional if you can refer to your "letter of April 6th" rather than something vague like your "letter of six or seven weeks ago."

If all of this sounds painfully fundamental, consider this: I received an important contract last week that was not dated. At the same time, I received a notice from the post office informing me that my address had been changed. Guess what? The post office forgot to include my revised zip code.

The bottom line to this is there are a lot of slipshod, ill-conceived things going on out there. Don't let your query letter fall into that category.

Now that we have the format nailed down, let's talk about how we go about writing the specific parts of the query letter. Let's start with the opening sentence: generally regarded in a business letter as the hook. Get straight to the point. Tell the person why you are writing the letter. The most effective style for a business letter is somewhere between "cute" and "rigor mortis."

Try this example for your opening:

My novel, *A Black River*, is available for your consideration. (Sounds stiff to me)

Or, how about:

The setting of my novel, *A Black River*, is the high country of the Sawtooth National Forest. (Better)

The second version added a mere seven words, but look at how much more information it gave the reader. Remember, one of the tests of a good business letter is this: Give the reader as much information as possible, using the fewest words possible.

Now we turn our attention to the synopsis (fiction) or proposal (non-fiction). The focus of your query letter is to describe

Getting Published

what you have written in 25 socko words. Why 25 words, you ask? Because you are busy and that agent or editor you are writing to is also a busy person. Plainly speaking, the essence of a good business letter (and that's exactly what your query letter is) is to give the individual the necessary information and then get out of the person's face. Editors, agents, all business people for that matter, appreciate not having their time impacted any more than necessary.

Trust me on this one. And, if you still doubt what I say, picture yourself at the local video store, trying to decide what movie to rent. How long does it take you? Answer: a few seconds – 17 on the average. You read the blurb on the front or back of the package, make your decision, and move on.

Fact: the agent or editor takes about that long to decide whether you have a good story or interesting proposal. While you may not think this is fair, it is reality. Knowing all of this should help you put that much-needed extra effort into the synopsis or proposal paragraph of your query letter.

Here is the synopsis paragraph I included in my query letter for *The Lake*.

The Lake is a horror novel set in a coastal resort village. It details the six days leading to a cataclysmic Labor Day disaster.

Did I capture the editor's interest? Let me put it this way – he was on the phone within two weeks asking for the manuscript. He bought it – and as this is being written, *The Lake* is in its third release.

Why did it work? Well, whether or not you think the micro synopsis portion of my letter is well written is a subject for another time. The point is it was sent to an editor that I knew worked for a publisher that printed a great many mass-market books with cataclysmic endings. It also told him the setting of the story (you can work a lot of themes and sub plots in a resort area setting), and that it covered a six-day period. The letter tells the agent or

SUBMISSION

editor that it will most likely be a fast-paced scenario and, therefore, a quick read.

Suffice to say, constructing a synopsis that encapsulates your novel and gives the agent or editor sufficient information (read that – creates enough interest) to keep them reading your query letter takes practice in tight writing.

Now comes the conclusion to your query letter. This part is simple. Just tell the agent or editor that the manuscript is complete and that you will send it immediately upon request. Tell them this, of course, only if it is true.

At this point, I feel compelled to tell you about the author in Iowa who had told two different editors that two different manuscripts were ready for submission. Both editors called her and wanted the manuscripts. She couldn't deliver. Her career is currently on hold while she tries to repair her damaged reputation with the publishing community.

Still with me? If you are – your query letter is done. Wrap it up. Sign off. Get out of the agent's or editor's face. Do not hinder your chances by telling the recipient of your query letter what a great novel you have written. Do not simper or beg. Never say something like "I hope you like it."

One final comment: Make your closing paragraph a positive one. If you say, "I look forward to hearing from you soon," you are letting the agent or editor know that you think your time is valuable too. I think it conveys just the right touch of author bravado.

The query letter is only part of the submission package – but it is clearly the most important part. Why? Because if you don't keep the reader interested, there is a good chance that the rest of your submission package just plain won't get read.

Lastly (is there such a word?), make certain you have included contact information. Even if it is personalized stationery that includes everything but your horsepower rating, it can't hurt to include your telephone number under your signature.

Getting Published

GENERAL BUSINESS LETTER FORMAT

>Your street address
City, State Zip Code
Date

Recipient's full name
Institution or title
Institution (if title above)
Street address
City, State, Zip Code

Recipient's name:

The first paragraph should be brief. It should be straight to the point. The recipient should be able to tell what the letter is about after reading the first paragraph. A guideline to authoring a tight and effective first paragraph of a business letter is to confine it to four sentences.

The second paragraph is broad in scope. Here is where you define the totality of the situation. Mention relevant background information. Explain or enlarge upon details that are important. Detail qualifications, authority, scope of matter. Where necessary, tie yourself to the matter being discussed. A tightly written second paragraph of a general business letter can usually be accomplished in six sentences.

The third paragraph you tie yourself, and/or your interest, to the situation that is the focus of your letter. *Focus* is key to a well-written business letter. Don't stray from the main purpose of your letter. Straying from the central point of your letter may confuse the reader about your purpose for writing. If you want the reader to take some action, spell it out. Be certain you have avoided ambiguity. If any paragraph of your letter is going to be lengthy, the third paragraph is where you go into detail. Still, I would caution you to guard against being wordy or redundant.

The fourth paragraph (not always necessary) is brief. What do you expect? Is the course of action clear? Don't dawdle. Thank the recipient for their time and consideration.

>Closing,
SIGNATURE
Keyboarded name

SUBMISSION

QUERY LETTER

Date
Person's Name
Title
Agency or Publisher's Company
Street Address
City, State Zip Code

Dear Mr. (Ms.) specific Name (1)

Deathscape is a horror novel focusing on a large scale ecological disaster. (2)

Deathscape takes place in a coastal resort village and details the events leading up to a cataclysmic Labor Day disaster in which thousands perish. (3)

An expanded synopsis of the manuscript is enclosed. The complete manuscript of *Deathscape* is available upon request. (4)

I look forward to your prompt response. (5)

Thank you for your time and interest. (6)

Signature

Enclosure

Getting Published

(1) The letter is directed to a specific individual.

(2) The hook sentence – it gets the reader into the letter.

(3) Your carefully constructed 25 to 30 word synopsis tells the editor or agent what your novel is all about.

(4) You tell the reader that if they are interested, the complete manuscript is available.

(5) A gentle but professional prod shows that you expect a prompt response.

(6) Common courtesy.

All of this, of course, is meticulously typed and edited, and sent out on your personalized stationery as part of your submission package which includes the resume and synopsis.

SUBMISSION

The Writer's Resume

A good submission package includes a relevant resume. Note, this is not comparable to your professional employment resume. This is your writer's resume.

First, let's talk about a work of fiction. Even if this is your first novel, you have had some writing experience: articles for the newspaper, copy for an advertising agency, a short story, working on the college newspaper, an organization newsletter, etc. Several years ago a lady came to one of my *How To Write a Novel* seminars and during the class introductions informed the rest of the attendees that she had been published 176 times. The rest of the attendees were in awe of her the entire day. At the close of the seminar I asked her about her obviously prolific writing career. That's when she confided that she had written 176 church bulletins – and every one of them was published.

Leave out personal items, like the fact that you are a den mother for 14 Cub Scouts, unless, of course, your novel just happens to be about a den mother of a group of Cub Scouts.

Remember, the key word is *relevant*.

Do include something like the fact that "my novel is set in Russia where I lived for five years." If your novel is a spy thriller and you were employed by the CIA, that's definitely relevant – include it. If the setting for your romance novel is Montana and you were born and raised in Montana, that's definitely relevant.

New writers tend to get a bit uptight when they think about putting a resume together for their first novel. Don't be. All that agent or editor is reading into that resume is the fact that you have writing experience. Besides, if they like your micro synopsis, your resume won't carry that much weight.

Let's turn our attention to the non-fiction proposal for a moment. It's been my experience that a resume carries a lot of weight when you are submitting a proposal. Here, your credentials are important and thus the resume receives decidedly more attention from the editor or agent. If you are an expert in a given field and

Getting Published

you are writing about a subject pertinent to that field, this is where you present your credentials.

In the case of my co-author, Dr. Earl Conn, on our book entitled *Effective Business Writing: Tight and Right*, his curriculum vitae (resume) gave a great deal of credence to that fact that we knew what we were talking about when we talked about business writing. This was augmented by the fact that I had spent 22 years in industry and had managed a sales force of 75 people. Relevant indeed.

One of the more interesting aspects of the non-fiction proposal, as compared to the fiction synopsis, is the fact that your credentials, in addition to being presented in the resume portion of your submission package, are incorporated a second time in the actual text of the proposal.

To defuse the specter of resume rigor mortis, I have included a copy of my own writer's resume, along with that of a young writer in Iowa who is just beginning his writing career.

The resume portion of your submission package can add a thoughtful and professional touch to your submission package if it is both relevant and tightly written – and that means never more than one page.

SUBMISSION

RESUME

PERSONAL:	Paul Macomber 1234 S. Fourth St. Davenport, IA 52800 (555) 555 – 1234
EDUCATION:	Attending University of Iowa, Iowa City, IA Graduate West High School, Davenport, IA
PROFESSIONAL:	Regular contributor to *Show and Tell* magazine for last two years Regular contributor to *Beak N'Eye* newspaper Author of over twenty short stories, including "Vacuums Can't Suck Paper Clips" which appeared in *Eyas* – short story anthology Completed Mississippi Valley Writers Conference Augustana College, Rock Island, IL
ACCOMPLISHMENTS:	Chosen to attend Creative Writing Workshop Augustana College, Rock Island, IL Awarded scholarship to attend Mississippi Valley Writers Conference Honor Roll and Perfect Attendance Awards West High School, Davenport, IA First Place – Science Fair – Recycling Division Entrant – *Parade Magazine* National Short Story Contest
PERSONAL:	Double Major in psychology and sociology at the University of Iowa, Iowa City, IA Amateur astronomer

Getting Published

THE MECHANICS OF WRITING A NOVEL

YOUR SEMINAR PRESENTER ...

R. Karl Largent, a.k.a. Robin Karl or Simon Lawrence, is an author, lecturer, and columnist who teaches writing at Tri State University. Before launching his writing and teaching careers, he spent 30 years in industry, the last 17 as VP of Marketing for an Indiana-based Fortune 500 multinational.

Largent brings an intriguing and varied collection of life experiences to his career as an author/lecturer. A former horse show judge and trainer of youth horses, he competed in SCCA road racing events, flew as a Weather Officer in the USAF, and served with the U.S. Weather Bureau.

Fiction works include:

SINISTER FICTION:	*BLACK DEATH* (1987)
	PAGODA (1990)
	ANCIENTS (1991)
	WITCH OF SIXKILL (1991)
	THE POND (1991)
	AMITYVILLE: THE NIGHTMARE CONTINUES (1992)
ADVENTURE:	*THE PROMETHEUS PROJECT* (1988)
	THE SEA (1999)
TECHNO-THRILLERS: (The Red Series)	*RED TIDE* (1993)
	RED ICE (1995)
	RED SKIES (1996)
	RED SAND (1997)
	RED WIND (1998)

SUBMISSION

Non-fiction works include:
A PONY IS NOT A BABY HORSE Pioneer Press 1982
GETTING STARTED: HANDBOOK FOR THE BEGINNING NOVELIST Powerhouse 1992
EFFECTIVE BUSINESS WRITING (co-authored with Dr. Earl Conn)
Pin & Pen Press 1994
THE JOB GAME (co-authored with Dr. Earl Conn) Pin & Pen Press 1994
GETTING PUBLISHED: HOW THE PROS DO IT
Robin Vincent Publishing 1999

An award-winning columnist with HNE, he has presented his seminars to over 3,000 writing hopefuls in workshops, classes, and conferences at various Indiana University regional sites, Western Michigan University, Ball State University, numerous Michigan community colleges, Augustana College, Rei State University, Anderson College, The Mississippi Valley Writers Conference, Midwest Writers Conference, the CIW, the RWA, and others.

He holds degrees from Saint Francis College, the University of Illinois, and Indiana University, was named Indiana's Columnist of the Year, and is the recipient of the Dorothy Hamilton Award for lifetime achievement.

Getting Published

The Expanded Synopsis

There are two schools of thought on this portion of your submission package. I have talked to a few writers who have been told to include the first three chapters of their novel when they contacted an agent or editor. If that's what they want, that's what you send them. In most cases, however, the agent or editor will want a synopsis. Why a synopsis? Because it is less time consuming for the recipient to read a 3 or 4 page synopsis than the 90 pages or so that constitute your first three chapters. (It's also less expensive for you.) The real reason most agents or editors want a synopsis is because they are looking for three things:

- They can determine if you have a whole story with a reader-grabbing ending.
- They can get an idea of where the novel can be slotted in their list of genres.
- They are checking out your writing style.

Sooner or later you will talk to someone who sold his or her novel without including an expanded synopsis along with their query letter. This is rare. Frankly, I can't imagine not doing it. If your query letter has generated interest, what do you think is going to happen if they have to call you and ask for more information? Are they still going to be interested five or six days later when your expanded synopsis hits their desk? Maybe. Maybe not. In a fast-paced publishing house, many things can happen in those five or six days. Why take the chance?

Now that you know *why* you should include your expanded synopsis, let's talk about *how* you write one.

Author James V. Smith Jr. has said that writing a synopsis is a whole lot like telling someone about the movie you saw the previous evening. You set the scene, identify the principal characters, describe the action, march through the story and, yes, you reveal that incredible, never before imagined, wholly original, spine tingling ending. If you don't, that agent or editor you are trying to

SUBMISSION

impress may think you haven't worked out the ending. Not including the climax is tantamount to saying, "I don't trust you." That is not a good way to start off a business relationship.

Writing an expanded synopsis demonstrates how well you are telling your story. So, include critical plot points, show the tensions and the conflicts. Everything I have stressed about the other components of your submission package applies here as well. Make your expanded synopsis as slick and polished as humanly possible.

Getting Published

SYNOPSIS

SYNOPSIS – RED SKIES
by R. Karl Largent

May 2, 1995

PREMISE

The premise of this book deals with a radical faction of the PRC (Peoples' Republic of China), known as the Fifth Academy (5A). 5A does not want the USA and Russia to continue to heal their philosophical, diplomatic and political differences. Reason: If that happens, the PRC will be the sole remaining stronghold of Communism in the world.

BACKGROUND

It is early August and there is a heat wave in Indianapolis. It is the eve of the **Brickyard 400,** the newest crown jewel in NASCAR's season long racing series. On a sultry, Saturday afternoon, over 300,000 people will gather in the famed Speedway to watch the race. Freeways are crowded, the city is jammed with racing fans, hotels and tourist attractions are taxed to capacity. People are edgy, nervous – attributed to the relentless heat wave, but also because 5A terrorists have warned that what happened in Great Britain and Mexico "could happen in the USA as well."

>   ... The Royal Opera House in London was bombed during a performance of Verdi's *Aida*, 267 died, 742 injured (June 16, birthday of the Queen). The Queen and her entourage left the opera house just moments before the explosion.
>   ... An off-shore oil rig is blown up off the coast of Mexico, kills 187, injures another 231 on May 5 (Cinco de Mayo). The Mexican President escapes leaving the rig just moments before the explosion.

SUBMISSION

Now Americans fear an attack. But we don't know where, we don't know when. We only know that we have been warned. The American President is planning to attend (note thread of continuity – heads of state) the **Brickyard 400** and the ISA is monitoring activity of known 5A sympathizers. (They are in the Indianapolis area.)

PROLOGUE

The prologue is the terrorist attack at the Indianapolis Motor Speedway during the **Brickyard 400**. Seventeen hundred people are killed, thousands are injured. (Prologue is lengthy; could be a first chapter by noting time delineation.)

THE STORY

Against this backdrop, the ISA (Internal Security Agency) is informed that an important Eastern Bloc aircraft designer, Milo Schubatis, is coming to the United States for an international conference. Schubatis is the man behind the Su-39 (comparable to our F-117). This is happening simultaneously with the defection of a Russian pilot with one of the two prototype Su-39 (NATO designation: Covert). He has defected to 5A. The Americans suspect this, but are unable to confirm it.

At the same time, ISA is alerted to a possible abduction plot of Schubatis by the 5A, located on the island of Hainan in south China.

ISA Chief, Clancy Packer, assigns T.C. Bogner responsibility for Schubatis' safety while he is in this country. On the way from the airport, the terrorists strike. The terrorists abduct Schubatis and leave the corpse of a badly burned Schubatis look-alike in his place. The bogus Schubatis' real identity is discovered during the ensuing autopsy.

Getting Published

5A manages to get the real Schubatis out of the country. Simultaneous with the discovery that Schubatis is still alive, American agents on Hainan report that they have discovered the whereabouts of the missing Su-39. Now it is clear what 5A is doing. They have the plane and the designer of the plane. They are now in a power position. When the ISA learns this, Bogner is dispatched to Hainan to recover Schubatis and, if possible, fly the Su-39 out of the 5A compound. If he cannot recover the Su-39, he has been instructed to destroy it (We learned earlier that the other Su-39 prototype has previously crashed and is destroyed).

Bogner's cover is as a Canadian arms dealer who is interested in doing business with the dissident 5A faction of the Red Army. He works with the US agent in Hainan, Shu Li, an attractive, American educated, Chinese national, who has contacts within the 5A compound of Danjia.

Meanwhile, his Chinese captors incarcerate an uncooperative Schubatis, still suffering from injuries in the terrorist attack. The leader of the 5A is Mao Quan, who has political ambitions to take over PRC leadership.

Bogner and Shu Li need help getting into the compound. They elicit the help of an aging Catholic priest who maintains an orphanage not far from the Danjia compound. The priest, with ties to the Chinese Nationalist Government on Taiwan, and with the aid of a former Chinese Nationalist pilot, has reassembled an old WW-II helicopter that is kept hidden and used to transport targets of 5A brutality to a small island off the coast of Hainan and eventual political asylum.

A two-stage plan is devised whereby they can get Schubatis out of the compound and at the same time destroy the Su-39. The mission is accomplished, but Colonel Mao Quan (the central antagonist and commanding officer of the 5A compound) discovers where they have taken Schubatis and orders his troops to recapture Schubatis and destroy the orphanage. The old priest is killed, but Bogner, Schubatis, and the young officer escape. When Quan learns this, he dispatches two Sukhoi Su-27 Flankers to abort Bogner's attempt to fly the helicopter to the small island that offers political asylum. Quan would rather have Schubatis dead than have the Russian live to reveal his plan to take over PRC leadership.

Bogner manages to destroy one of the 5A's pursuing planes, but the helicopter is hit, crashes on the small island, and the remaining Flanker fires missiles at the downed helicopter. From the ground, Bogner manages to destroy the remaining Su-27. They have escaped (only temporarily).

But Quan is not done. He learns how the Americans plan to get Schubatis off the island and leads a death squad to finish the job. There is a final assassination attempt at the docks where the Americans have made arrangements to pick up Bogner, Schubatis, and the young Chinese officer. The attempt fails and Quan flees.

The trio boards an old freighter that will take them to Macao where they will catch a flight back to the states. But Quan has secretly boarded the freighter (it is now a personal vendetta and Quan is out of control) where there will be a final confrontation. Quan kills Schubatis. Bogner kills Quan.

As the book ends, Bogner is standing in the airport at Macao. He is reporting in to Packer. The Su-39 is destroyed and the man who designed and built it is dead. The mission is both a success ... and a failure.

Getting Published

The Non-Fiction Book Proposal

The non-fiction book proposal is an entirely different breed of cat. There are very few similarities between the synopsis and the proposal except that each is considered part of the submission package. Perhaps the most significant difference is that many first non-fiction book proposals are submitted before the book is actually written. That is seldom (read that 'hardly ever') the case when it comes to a first novel.

A proposal is very carefully segmented and, although the book may not actually be written at this point, much, if not most, of the work has already been done. The author must be able to discuss in depth: where the book will be slotted, the identity of other books on the same subject and how they are sold, and what new information is being presented. In the market analysis section of the proposal, that information must be presented by title, author and publisher.

Let's look at the anatomy of a proposal. A proposal:
- Has a cover page.
- Contains a detailed overview of the contents of the manuscript.
- Contains a market analysis.
- Contains a credentials section.
- Contains an outline or an index for each chapter of the book.

The cover page should include the title of the work, the names of the authors and the name of the agent, if you have selected one. In this section, I have included an unedited model of the proposal for *Effective Business Writing: Tight and Right* to show how a proposal can be laid out.

On the Overview page, Dr. Conn and I explain what our book is all about and we march the editor or agent right through the book, section by section. Much of what is included on this page of the proposal is lifted from our notes, discussions about what should be included in the content of the book and a rough draft.

In the second page of our proposal, we covered the market analysis. This is grunt work — but it must be done to show the agent or editor where you are positioned in time and space and the market place. A note of caution here: If there are already a number of books

SUBMISSION

on the same subject currently available to the book buying public, you must show how your effort differs. Fail to do this and you are doomed. Think about it – how many books are available on the assassination of John Kennedy? If you can't point out the difference between your effort and those that are already available, the chances of getting your book published are thin indeed.

From the market analysis section, we turn our attention to the credentials. Here all that is required is defining why you are qualified to write the book on the subject you are proposing. If you are proposing an authoritative work on terrorist activities, tell the editor or agent how and why you know so much about the subject of terrorism. The same would be applicable to books on subjects such as raising cattle or building clocks. If the tie-ins are vague – elaborate. However, don't drone on with qualifications that are irrelevant. Example: The fact that I served some 22 years as Vice President of Marketing of a Fortune 500 multinational is not really relevant. The fact that I had to communicate (mostly in writing) with a sales force that covered the entire country is relevant.

Needless to say, a good proposal emerges only after you have your book well thought out (or written) and after you have edited and revised your proposal until it shines like spun gold.

Having completed all of the above, you now come to a fork in the road with your non-fiction proposal.

If the book is written, you can (and probably should) give a chapter by chapter breakdown of your work. One editor I talked to said he liked to see a layout of the chapters. In this case, a short paragraph, eight to ten sentences detailing what is in each chapter, is appropriate.

For works that are still in the 'thinking" stage, a proposed outline may be appropriate. This is the way Dr. Conn and I chose to present our proposal. Note, however, that the outline is complete right down to the number of pages per index category.

Now you're ready to put all of these components: The query letter, the resume, and your expanded synopsis or proposal together into one envelope. In that same envelope, include a self-addressed,

Getting Published

stamped envelope (SASE), take it to the post office, making certain you have the proper postage on your mailing envelope and your return package, and mail it.

Mark the date you mailed it on your calendar, because you will be convinced they have had your package four months when, in fact, it has only been four weeks. Allow for the fact that mail doesn't always get there as fast as you had hoped it would, that the editor or agent to whom you sent your package may be out of the country, or even home having a baby. Despite convincing arguments and opinions to the contrary, editors are human and agents are interested in developing writers.

How long do you wait before you follow up? That varies. If you are working with an agent, you are probably going to get an indication of how they feel about your work in four to six weeks. Some agents take longer. If you sent your submission package to an editor at a publishing house, the wait is probably going to be twice as long (at least). With publishers, rejections can come thundering back in two or three weeks or crawling back in four months. The flip side is, if the agent or editor wants to see your manuscript, you'll probably get a phone call. If that happens, run, sprint, dart, bolt, tear, and burn up the road to get the manuscript in the mail.

I wouldn't be doing my job if I didn't pass on this observation: Don't assume that all editors and agents are good at their job. You'll find all levels of performance and competence in the publishing business.

A final comment on the submission package. If you have decided to try to market your manuscript through an agent, you should submit your work to only one agent at a time. Offer exclusive rights to market your material. If the agent turns you down, go to the next one on your list. Editors frequently work with multiple submissions. They are used to seeing authors change publishers. The right agent will be with you for the long run.

Sounds like a lot of work? It is. But, you can enhance your odds of selling your manuscript if you prepare a truly professional submission package.

SUBMISSION
PROPOSAL

Proposal for

*Effective Business Writing:
Tight and Right*

by
Dr. Earl Conn
Dean, School of Communication
Ball State University
and
R. Karl Largent
former V.P. Marketing
Arvin Industries

Agent:
Barbara Beman Puechner
"The Peekner Literary Agency, Inc."
3121 Portage Rd.
Bethlehem, PA 18017
610-974-9158

Getting Published

OVERVIEW

The first page of a non-fiction proposal should be an overview of the material you intend to cover in your book.

Example from: *Effective Business Writing: Tight and Right*

Methods of communicating information come and go. Who can say how we will transmit business information ten, even five years from now? But one thing remains certain: Whatever the method, the ability to prepare that information clearly and in a readable format will not change.

That's what *Effective Business Writing: Tight and Right* is all about. We have one goal. That goal is to accelerate your continuing preparation for effective business writing. No matter where you or we stand in this endeavor, we can always learn more about doing it better. Both authors have been in the writing business for decades, but it's accurate to say we learn every day. Sound like an exaggeration? Believe us, it isn't.

This workbook is a step in that direction. It is divided into four parts:

Part I, "Getting Ready To Write," emphasizes the crucial point that thinking needs to precede writing. Writing is like life. The better prepared you are before you start, the more success you can expect. So thinking about what you are going to write is critical.

Part II, "The Mechanics of Writing," frankly, may be more than you want to know right now about grammar and language usage. But it's there if you need it. We've tried to stick to the basics.

Part III, "Internal Documents," and Part IV, "External Documents," are built around our thesis that the special difference in these two types of documents is *audience*, not writing style. What does the audience already know? What do they need to know?

SUBMISSION

What is your goal in reaching this particular audience? These are the questions that matter.

Effective Business Writing: Tight and Right was originally conceived as a quick learning tool for professionals and people promoted into positions of responsibility where the rigors and rules of writing had become vague. We believe it serves that purpose and more.

We invite you to read on ... and become a better business writer.

MARKET ANALYSIS

The next section of your non-fiction proposal should be a market analysis of books currently on the market that cover the same subject. In this section you discuss when these books were published. You should address such questions as how well they are selling, when they were published, whether or not they are still available ... and most importantly, how your book differs from these previously published works. What is new and different about your book? You will also want to point out why you believe your book will have more appeal for readers than other books on the same subject. Did you put a different spin on the subject? What new information are you sharing?

Discuss competing books by title, author, and publisher.

CREDENTIALS

This is a very straightforward section. Why are you qualified to write this book? If your work is co-authored, obviously, both authors should elaborate on their qualifications. This is not the place to be timid or shy. Spell out the successes in your background as they relate to the subject matter.

In *Effective Business Writing: Tight and Right*, Earl Conn pointed out that he was Dean of the School of Communications at Ball State University and served as Chairman of the BSU School

Getting Published

of Journalism for over twenty years. He mentioned the fact that he had written for numerous trade journals, newspapers, and had interviewed celebrities including James Dean, Julie Andrews, and others.

The co-author, Largent, focused on the fact that he was Vice President of Marketing for a multinational, responsible for product sales, developing new markets, product introductions, and the care and management of twenty internal sales people as well as seventy-five field sales personnel. Largent also elaborated on the fact that he teaches business communications for a private university.

The Credentials section must be presented in a tightly written manner. Don't drone on with qualifications that are irrelevant. But do remember to mention your academic credentials.

At this point in your non-fiction book proposal, you have an option:

1. You may wish to outline the chapters of your book, pointing out the key points of each chapter
or
2. You may wish to present the publisher with an index of the material you are covering.

In the case of *Effective Business Writing: Tight and Right*, we included a copy of the actual index page as we envisioned it.

Note: We used our computer to actually lay out how we saw the index appearing in the manuscript. We did this by taking the manuscript to a copy house and having it reproduced.

SUBMISSION

TABLE OF CONTENTS

i. **Preface**

Part One – Getting Ready to Write
- 3   What's Happening Here?
- 4   Help Is On The Way
- 6   Think – What Do We Mean By 'Thinking'
- 9   First You Think, Then You Write
- 10   The Plan
- 13   The Content
- 14   First You Think, Then You Write: Summary
- 15   Worthwhile Content
- 18   Worthwhile Content: Summary
- 19   Logical Organization
- 22   Logical Organization: Summary
- 23   Tight Writing Drill
- 24   A Clear and Readable Style
- 25   Style Tips
- 27   Helpless Words
- 28   A Clear and Readable Style: Summary
- 29   Tight Writing Drill
- 30   A Wrap-Up To Part One

Part Two – The Mechanics of Writing
- 33   A Quick Refresher In Business Writing Mechanics
- 36   Sentences
- 39   The Simple Sentence
- 40   The Compound Sentence
- 41   The Complex Sentence/The Compound-Complex Sentence
- 42   Recognizing Different Kinds of Sentences
- 43   Sentences Summary/Paragraphs
- 44   The Nature of Paragraphs/Paragraphs Should Be Focused
- 45   Paragraphs Should be Carefully Developed
- 46   Paragraphs Should Be Tightly Written

Getting Published

47	Paragraphs Should Be Well Organized
48	Paragraphs Should Be Coherent
49	Finally, A Potpourri Of Paragraph Paradigms
50	Paragraphs: Summary
51	Editing And Revision
52	Editing And Revision: Summary/Learning To Edit: Examples
55	Wordiness And Editing: Summary/Tight Writing Drill
56	The Art Of Using Plain English
58	Numbers, Units, and Other Technical Stuff
59	Let's Talk Numbers
60	Let's Talk Units of Measure
61	Something To Talk About/Our Top 10 Rules For Solving Grammar and Punctuation Problems

Part Three – INTERNAL DOCUMENTS

67	Before We Begin, A Couple Of Distinctions
68	Internal Documents
69	The Memo/Formatting The Memo: Evident'Or Subtle'
70	The Evident'Memo: Get To The Point
71	More About Memos
72	The Subtle'Memo: The Gentle Art Of Persuasion/Mechanical And Formatting Guides
74	The Evident'Memo Format
75	The Subtle'Memo Format/A Seldom Used Third
76	The Memo: Summary
77	A Different Kind Of 'Internal' Document: The Report
79	The First Distinction
80	Everything Starts With Thinking
82	Organize Your Data Gathering
83	Formatting The Formal Business Report
84	The Memo of Transmittal
85	The Cover Page
87	The Executive Summary
88	The Text Or Body Of The Report
89	Introduction/The Body Of The Document

SUBMISSION

90	The Conclusion/Summary, Conclusion ... Which?
91	Maybe A Recommendation?/Exhibits
92	Glossary
93	Finally, The Bibliography/The Report: Summary
95	Visual Aids
96	Some Comments About Electronic Mail

Part Four – External Documents

101	Let's Talk About External Documents
102	Getting Focused
103	The Parts Of A Typical Business Letter
104	The Date/Inside Address Or Contact Information
105	About the Address Of The Recipient
106	The Salutation
107	The Closing
110	Final Comments On The Business Letter Format/Finally, Letter Appearance and Forms
111	Edit, Edit, Edit, Edit, And, If Necessary, Revise/Some Valid Generalizations About Business Letters
112	Effectiveness Of Your Letter
113	From Neutral Content To Matters Of 'Yes' And 'No'
114	The 'No' Letter
118	The 'Specific Interest' Letter
119	Interesting? To Do That, Start With Tone/Sincerity Is Vital
120	Be Conversational, Write Casually
121	Every Business Letter Should Try To Create Good Will
122	And Finally
125	Identifying With Your Reader
126	Individuate Your Reader
127	Inure Your Reader/The Last Word

Part Five – Practice Drills

131	Exercises

147	**Afterword**

Getting Published

AGENTS

If someone were to ask me to list the five most frequently asked questions at one of my writing seminars or classes on writing, one of them would certainly be:

Question: Should I get an agent before I write my book – or should I wait until after I have written the book and then look for an agent?
Answer: Write the novel. Then worry about agents. If you are planning a non-fiction work, you can try contacting the agent or publisher first. (If you are confused, go back and re-read the section on the Submission Package.)

Let's assume, however, that you have decided to work with an agent. Fact: Literary agents make money only when they sell a literary property. Editors rely on agents to send on publishable, professional material. In other words, the agent is putting their reputation on the line by making a value judgement about the work. In effect, your agent is telling the editor, "I know the caliber of work you buy, I know what you're looking for, and I know the degree of excellence you demand in manuscripts. I've taken all of this into consideration and believe this work may meet your needs."

Question: Do you mean an agent might *not* send out my work?
Answer: Absolutely. To an agent, your work is business.

An agent who sends an editor a manuscript that is below par is in danger of jeopardizing a business relationship with that editor. Which is why a good agent is reluctant to take on new writers until they have proven they can do what they say they will do. Agents (as well as editors) know all too well that many books are started but all too few are finished.

AGENTS

Question: How will I know if my book is ready to submit?
Answer: You'll have to trust your agent to determine that.

The agent serves another purpose in the publishing cycle. A good agent will read, assess, and often recommend changes before submitting a work. Mine does. When I send a manuscript to New York, my agent gives it a thorough read and then discusses with me the changes he believes the manuscript needs to enhance his chances of selling the work.

Reality check: Your agent and editor will decide whether your work is of a sufficient commercial quality so that people will pluck it from the bookshelves and *buy* it.

Question: How can I judge an agent's performance?
Answer: The same way you judge any other professional you decide to work with.

More reality: Not all agents are effective. In my first life, 25 years spent in industry, I worked with manufacturer's agents. The principle is the same as in the publishing industry; only the product is different. I learned that there were as many different performance levels of agents as with employees. Some agents work hard; others don't. Some agents have two or three major lines (authors), and some have many. If an agent has two or three major authors who generate ample income, he can afford to take on some new writers until they become income producers for the agency. Or, he can baby-sit his income-producers and not even worry about developing new authors.

Some agencies represent many authors. I talked to one who claims to represent 153. If all those authors are active, producing one, and in some cases, two works a year, that's one busy agency where no one – except the top income producers – get much attention. But if half of those 153 authors are

Getting Published

producing a manuscript every five years or so, the day-to-day workload of that agency may be greatly diminished.

Like life, situations vary. A literary agent who is perfect for me may not be the right one for you. When your submission package is ready, shop around. Face it, you would have to do the same thing if you were hiring an accountant or lawyer. Whatever you do, don't choose an agent who charges you a fee to read your work before agreeing to represent the manuscript in question.

Question: What's the secret to selling an unfinished novel on the basis of a synopsis?
Answer: Easy. Sell your finished first novel first – then you'll have a track record.

Follow the rules to sell your first book whether it's fiction or non-fiction. If it does well, then you'll have a good chance of selling your second effort with either a synopsis or proposal. (And sample chapters if required).

We've all heard stories about the first novel that sold based on an idea scratched out on a napkin over a two-Perrier lunch. Well, I fear that, for the most part, that's all they are – stories. In the fifteen years that I have been associated with writers, I've only known one person that sold a novel based on an idea. And that individual had already achieved celebrity status in another arena. Agents, editors, and publishers are interested in complete novels – finished – wrapped up – with a bow around them. Why? Because that is the true test of the novice novelist: Can he or she sustain the effort it takes to complete the work— at the same high competency level throughout the entire novel. Keep in mind, and agents and editors know this, thousands, maybe hundreds of thousands of novels are started each year. Note: I said started. How many are finished? No one knows because most of them never see the light of day.

AGENTS

At the risk of sounding redundant. It's a whole different scenario if you plan on doing a non-fiction work. In the case of non-fiction, you can approach an agent (or publisher) with a proposal. But that proposal needs to be thorough, well thought out, and meticulously presented. Plus, the writer who is proposing the work, should be a real authority on the subject. Suffice to say, of the five non-fiction works that I have been involved with, four of the five were written before I even approached the subject of having them published.

Reality Check: Don't go agent hunting until you have written your novel and polished it to perfection.

Question: I've heard that I can't get an agent until I'm published – and I can't get published until I have an agent. What do I do?
Answer: Stop worrying.

You can relieve your anxiety by purchasing a copy of Jeff Herman's *Insiders' Guide to Book Editors, Publishers, and Literary Agents* or the current edition of *Writers' Market* published by Writer's Digest Books. Pick out some agencies, review what kinds of books they handle, how many clients they have, etc. If an agency offers free information about how to make submissions to them, by all means grab it.

Look at it this way: This is no different than the rest of the research you've had to accomplish to complete your manuscript.

One piece of advice that I've heard every successful author give when asked about agents is this: Do not call an agent and begin a long, rambling, disjointed conversation about your plot, telling how original, creative, and well-written your work is. If you do, you're dead.

Find out how to make a submission, follow all the guidelines, and send the manuscript. Let the manuscript speak for itself.

Getting Published

Question: What's my number one worry in dealing with an agent?
Answer: Yourself.

I asked a literary agent what his major objection was to working with new writers. His answer was succinct:
"Lack of professionalism."
He then went on to recite the blunders he associates with new writers:
"They take up too much time on the telephone. They ramble on, wasting time with small talk, looking for positive reinforcement about their writing, hoping to say something that will make me give extra attention to their work. Hell, when I'm in the office, I'm on the telephone working the publishers for my authors. I have a window of about four hours a day when editors are willing to accept calls. I can't be wasting precious phone time holding someone's hand."

Question: What if my book doesn't sell?
Answer: Write another one – a better one.

If your work is worthy of being published – it will be published. Agents, editors, and publishers need manuscripts. It's that old better *mousetrap* principle.

How to Approach an Agent – Plan A

Let's say your novel is finished and you have identified two or three literary agencies that you believe are the kinds of agency that you want to represent you. Under these circumstances, here are some viable options:

• **Call the agency and verify the name of the individual** in that agency to whom you want to send your manuscript. Verify the spelling of the individual's name and that the person is still with the agency. Also verify whether or not that agent is willing

AGENTS

to work with an unpublished author. If you are fortunate enough to get an affirmative response, thank the person on the other end of the line and hang up. Do not try to engage the person in chitchat (be professional – you got what you came for). Assume that the person you are talking to is busy. (If the person isn't busy, this may not be the agent you are looking for.)

- **Prepare a professional submission package** that includes the query letter, your resume, and synopsis (fiction) or proposal (non-fiction). If the agency has indicated they want sample chapters, by all means, comply with their requirements.
- **Send the package** and give the agency at least 10 days before you make the second call. In that call, all you are doing is verifying that they have received your submission package. *Do not ask* what they think of it; they may not have read it yet. I can assure you, if the agency is hot for your idea, there will be an appropriate expression of interest. If not, they will tell you. If the latter is the case, you've just saved yourself a fist full of dollars in postage costs by not sending the entire manuscript.

I received a phone call not long ago from a friend who had just been informed that the agent he selected was not interested in representing his work. He was crestfallen. He shouldn't have been. That rejection does not necessarily mean that the agent doesn't like his writing. A refusal to handle a particular work may simply mean the agency is already representing a similar work or an author with a similar style, that the subject is not currently a hot market, or any one of a hundred other valid business reasons. A rejection is nothing more than an expression of *"no interest at this time"* or *"no interest by this agent or agency."* That's all it is. In most cases it is not a judgment of the work unless the agent actually tells you that he or she feels your writing (or the plot, or the characters) needs further development.

Getting Published

Question: I've been rejected; what do I do now?
Answer: Simple, select another agency and repeat the entire process.

- **Start by sending a fresh (clean) copy of your submission package** to the next agency on your list. Make it as sparkling as that first submission. Retain the original and take some patience pills. The wait is on – again. Make your call after 10 days to make certain they have received your submission package. Agents have to read manuscripts to know what they have and think about where to market them. Reading manuscripts takes time.
- **Call the agency after 10 weeks if you haven't heard anything.** In the publishing business, 10 weeks is not an unreasonable time. If they tell you they are not interested, don't whimper and ask why – in all likelihood they'll tell you why they aren't interested. This may be a little hard to swallow, but it may give you a clue about something that needs to be adjusted (read that, fixed) before you submit your package to someone else.

If you are turned down several times in a row, you should probably start questioning the appeal or quality of your work.

How to Approach an Agent – Plan B

Several aspiring writers I know have tucked their manuscript under their arm and hustled off to a writer's conference because they know the conference committee has invited an agent to attend the conference for the specific purpose of meeting new authors. If you dislike the idea of sending your manuscript to someone you don't know, or are having difficulty connecting with an agent, you may wish to give this strategy a try.

In this case, the chances are excellent that you can arrange to have a face-to-face with a real live agent. In all probability it will be a brief encounter (every unpublished writer at a conference wants to meet an agent). Your meeting with that agent may even

AGENTS

happen in a group setting, but it will be a chance to have your work reviewed by a professional – and just maybe, if that agent isn't interested in representing you, he or she may know of an agent that would be right for you.

You may well be asking what you've gained by this extra time and expense for a long shot. Well, for one thing, that agent has a face to tie with the name – and the agent knows you are serious enough about your work to invest time and money to come and meet her. One other thing, you have now met an agent – and that perspective of the agent as some sort of *another world creature* is a little less daunting.

Let me stress something here. Deal with agents one at a time. Do not send a copy of your manuscript to two different agents at the same time. By the same token, do not send a copy of your manuscript to an agent and a publisher at the same time – you may get yourself in a box. If you're going to work with an agent, let that agent decide who sees your manuscript first.

Finally, I would be remiss if I did not point this out again. To you, your manuscript is a work of art, something very personal. To everyone else involved in the publishing industry it is a product for sale in a business – a tough business. On the other hand, if your work is high quality, someone will want to buy it, and someone will want to represent it. Agents make money when they sell a work. Publishers are in the business of selling books. Bottom line: The system works. By becoming a true professional who consistently turns out high caliber work, you can become part of the system.

Getting Published

MAKING A LIVING AS A WRITER
by Alan Garinger

Somewhere along the line, everyone who writes wonders if he or she can make a living doing it. The simple answer to that is "Yes, you can." A more accurate answer is "Yes, you can if ... "

I have observed a few differences between writing because you have to (the compulsion) and writing because you **have** to (to make a living). There is a difference between being a "private" writer and being a "public" or professional writer.

This evolution is best described by the French playwright Moliere, "Writing is a lot like prostitution. First you do it because you like it. Then you do it for a few friends. Then you do it for money." So much for romance.

Going "public" requires a certain unromantic mindset, a special attitude that is observable in everyone I know who writes for a living. It is especially obvious among free-lance (self-employed) writers. When you first discover it, it seems too subtle as to be insignificant.

I've heard private writers say, "I'm going to spend more time with my writing." Now, it's okay to say, "I'm going to spend more time with my children." It's even okay to say, "I'm going to spend more time with my pancreas."

But to say, "I'm going to spend more time with **my** writing" puts ownership in the wrong place for a public writer. When you go public it isn't **your** writing any longer. You aren't writing for yourself. You are writing for an audience.

Many private writers are unwilling to give up ownership. This reluctance manifests itself in all sorts of paranoia. I know private writers who maintain so much ownership in what they write that they won't submit manuscripts for publication because they fear someone will steal their ideas. Frankly, I've never written anything that was so wonderful that anyone would want to steal it. In fact, I'd be flattered if someone did.

Getting Published

Making a living by writing presupposes publication, not just once in a while, but almost every time out. This thought alone has a negative karma for most private writers. They think their "Art" is subverted by the quest for profit. To them, cash equates to crass. Public writers don't see it that way.

One more observation before I get to my One Rule for making a living writing – you must be prepared to be extremely productive. You will need to produce more volume than you ever expected you could. You will need to be prepared to write all manner of things, perhaps from several genre. You may be called upon to write for media you had never thought of. In other words, you need to have enough confidence in yourself to believe you can write anything. You have to be ready to say, "Yes, I can do that project" whatever the offer might be.

I've had some wonderful adventures by getting in over my head and having to dig my way out. As a result, I've written everything from cartoon quips to scholarly books. I've done textbooks on science and math and promotional copy for a pizza company. I've written television programs, computer software and novels. Being versatile is an important part of public writing.

Keep this statistic in mind as you consider what your writing career will look like. Eighty percent of people who say they want to write for a living want to do fiction, where only twenty percent of the writing jobs are. That means that the remaining twenty percent of the "wannabes" have an option on eighty percent of the paying jobs. Incidentally, poets don't generally expect to make a living writing poetry, so they don't figure in this equation.

Now for my **One Rule** for making a living writing:

Treat writing as if it's a business.

Because it is. This means that you make decisions on what and how to write from a business standpoint and not an emotional one. What you write is your product (Oh, no! My art,

MAKING A LIVING

my emotion, my blood, sweat, and tears, my soul is merely a product?). You must spend your time working on those projects that will sell. It would be really dumb for a store to stock things that no customer would buy. Stores that do this don't stay in business very long.

Furthermore, you will need to work as hard at a writing business as you would with any small business you might start. Keep in mind that small businesses fail for two major reasons: (1) lack of capital; (2) lack of focus. The writing business is no different.

According to photojournalist Bill Thomas, you need to have enough **capital reserve** to be able to live for two years before you quit your day job. There are more than just living expenses. I spend over a thousand dollars a year just for postage and copies of manuscripts that shuttle back and forth through the mail – twice that for the telephone.

You may think you are a complete writer, but I doubt it. No one is. I hire editors, researchers, artists and secretaries from time to time. I'm very good at some parts of the writing business. I'm not good at all at others. I hire people who know more than I do about some things.

If you're in business, you can't rely on friends to evaluate your work. If you were in the house painting business, would you ask your friends to come out on the job to evaluate how you're doing? Probably not. Why would you think that your writing business is any different?

Add to this the length of time between starting a project and having a marketable, income-generating product, and you can see the need for capital reserves. Writing isn't a good way to turn a fast buck.

So, you need a certain amount of capital and some business savvy.

Focus is equal in importance. There are certain luxuries a private writer has that a public writer doesn't. Simply being able to experience "writer's block" is a private writer's advantage. Public writers can't afford writer's block.

Getting Published

One of the best ways I have found to beat writer's block is to get a contract before you write. I can't overemphasize this point. When I quit my day job to go into writing full time, I promised myself that I would never write anything unless I had a contract in my hand. I've been pretty successful at that, with a couple of glaring exceptions – both of which were financial disasters.

If you have a contract, all those things you now worry about are meaningless. You have a specified deadline and you've got to meet it. Writer's block and all those other constraints have no place in this scenario. Producing within a given time frame is a crucial part of the writing industry. This is also the way to establish a reputation. If you can produce under pressure, the word gets around.

The "get a contract first" precept does not mean that you haven't already researched, written sample portions, studied the markets and analyzed every part of the project. The most successful writers get jobs by submitting proposals for the work they do writing the project itself.

There are several books based on this premise which you may want to study. What they will all tell you is that the killer proposal is simply a good sales pitch. It sells the work to a publisher or client, but perhaps more importantly, it sells *you* as a competent professional.

The guideline is this: It's better to spend three months developing a proposal and not be able to sell the work than to work three years completing the work and not be able to sell it.

Your focus needs to be on your audience and on developing material that does the job that your readers (viewers, users, clients) want done. The job may enlighten, educate, inform, entertain or scare the pants off them. The best way I've found to maintain this focus is to treat every job as if it is a problem-solving activity. This requires analyzing everything you do. Ask yourself these questions (among others you will develop):

MAKING A LIVING

1. What is this project supposed to do? (And for whom does it do it?)
2. Does it do it in the best way possible?
3. Does it have a beginning, a middle, and an end?
4. How many words can I take out of it and still do the job?
5. Are the transitions smooth?

Despite this somewhat self-conscious process, the writing still must be lively. As author Gary Provost says, "You've got to take out the boring stuff." All those writing skills you practiced when you were a private writer take on a new, wide-eyed reality when your livelihood depends on how well you execute them.

You might think that if you write day in and day out for years it becomes a mechanical, dreaded chore. Well, it can, and for some people it does. They are the ones who leave the business. The attrition rate among producing writers is astounding.

If you love the writing business and want to continue doing it, you must keep the magic touch with words. You must cherish the thrill you get when you write that well-turned phrase. But as a public writer, it must send chills up the spine of the audience as well. Here is how you do that.

You have to do your **finger exercises**. Novelist Harry Mark Petrakis uses the analogy of a concert pianist. He says that no self-respecting concert musician would think of performing unless she or he had spent several hours with finger exercises. He thinks it is audacious for writers to believe that they can just sit down at the keyboard and perform for their audience without this preparation.

Figure out what works for you. Here's what I do. I'm usually working on more than one project at a time. Depending on deadlines, one of them I'm doing as a performance, I'm doing another as finger exercises. That is, I open up my mind and let the words roll. I have dozens of such finger exercises files that don't fit any active project. I review them from time to time to see what I can use.

Getting Published

Once in a while, there is enough material accumulated to become a saleable project. *The Random Plotter*, a computer software that helps writers develop fiction plots, is an example. Because I had to learn how to program computers in order to write computer courseware, I needed to keep at it or I would forget how to do it. This project was a result of the finger exercises I did to keep the computer language firmly implanted in my mind. You may think you would never forget how to write, and you're right. But you **can** lose your sparkle.

I find a good deal of inspiration in doing research. You may think that if you're doing fiction, it all comes out of your head, so why do research? Frankly, there's not that much in my head, and I'm suspicious of those writers who claim that they just sit down and their muse takes the wheel. I don't believe it. I recommend doing a lot of what I call "sensuous research," no matter what you write.

Sensuous research, by my definition, means that you make the effort to experience what you're writing about. If you're writing about a Head Start class, go sit in a tiny chair and listen to the four-year-olds. If you're writing about life in a nursing home, go have lunch with the residents. Even if you're drawing from your own history, it's important to refresh your outlook through new or renewed experiences. You should already have done the library or encyclopedic research before you start a project. But this alone isn't enough.

James Alexander Thom (*Follow the River, From Sea to Shining Sea, Children of First Man*) is the best example I know of a writer who is expert at this kind of research. He does outrageous things to experience what his characters had to face. Once he was writing about the capture of Sackville, and his characters had to wade the Wabash River at flood time. He didn't know if this was possible, so he waited for a flood and did it. If you read Thom's works, you realize the importance

MAKING A LIVING

of this closeness to one's characters. He has the ability to make his characters hurt like no one else I know.

To write convincingly, you need to know something. In fact, you need to know more about what you write than anyone else does. When you put that first word on the page, it has to be there with **authority** or no one will listen. You have to know your story and characters and settings better than anyone else.

Stories come from what you know, and the story's the whole thing. Don't kid yourself; this rule applies to everything you write, not just fiction. You may be developing some esoteric treatise of the most scholarly nature. If there's no story, forget it.

If you are in the business of writing, you must continually look for new products. This requires as much effort as it does in any business. Without new products, businesses fail. Since a writer's product comes out of the warehouse of his or her head, continually updating the inventory is mandatory.

Along with knowing something comes the need to develop a **specialty**, something you know more about than anyone else. In the writing business, you need to hack out your niche. A specialty helps you establish yourself as a serious member of the writing industry.

The business of writing has been good to me financially. It has taken me to three continents. It has allowed me to meet thousands of fascinating people. Writing for instructional television has made it possible for me to "do well by doing good." Writing for young people has restored a measure of my youth.

Still, it's a lonely business. At some point, every project is a solitary activity. You must continually remind yourself that everything you write is important to somebody. In all of this talk about marketing and publishing, writing is still paramount. Most of the things you think publishing will do for you, it won't. It won't make you prettier, or smarter, or more famous, or even richer, probably. It will make you a living if you work hard enough.

Getting Published

**Four things you can do next week
to get started in the writing business**

1. If you haven't done so already, start a checking account in the name of your writing business.

2. Get some letterhead and business cards printed with your company name.

3. Establish a work routine that includes a writing project and finger exercises.

4. Tell everyone you know that you're in the writing business. This is almost as good as a contract. It makes you prove it.

**Five things you can do next month
to get your writing business moving**

1. Get a contract. This doesn't have to be for the great American novel.
   Talk to the local newspaper about a feature you can write.
   Write an article for your church magazine or company newsletter.
   Develop a flyer for a store's grand opening.
   Don't forget about the possibility of doing research for other writers.

2. Find your specialty (if you don't already know it). This doesn't have to be grandiose; it just has to be identifiable. Spend some time every day refining it.

3. Make outlines for three projects you could do that relate to your specialty. Check writers' market guides for potential sales.

4. Start your "Lifetime Accomplishments Want List."

MAKING A LIVING

Fill it with your ideas, dreams, visions – all those things you're going to do. This list should grow every day. Make it so long that you'd have to live two hundred years to do it all.

5. Keep putting as much financial reserve as you can afford into your business account.

Four things you can do in the next year to solidify your writing business

1. Get a contract.

2. Get another contract.

3. Attend a writers' conference.
   This gives you the opportunity to meet other people who write. You won't think you're so strange when you realize that others share your dream.

4. Get to know the people in the industry who can make your business work. You should be on a first name basis with editors, publishers, producers, agents, and several successful writers. The publishing industry is a massive network. People in the industry know each other. They need to know you if you are to succeed.

Four things you can do the rest of your life that keep your business going

1. Enjoy it – you're doing what you love.

2. Think more about your contributions than the money you make.

3. Encourage other writers.

4. Write every day. And keep writing.

Getting Published

Biting my truant pen, beating myself for spite:
Fool!' said my Muse to me, look in thy heart and write.'
                    Astrophel and Stella, Sonnet 1

... MORE THOUGHTS ON HOW TO MAKE A BUCK OR TWO BY WRITING
by R. Karl Largent

Although they are not necessarily synonymous, some words tend to be connected in some ethereal and yet pragmatic way to our thoughts about becoming a "full-time" writer.

Take "living" for example. The question always arises, "Can I make a living as a full-time writer?"

Another word is "money." "What kind of money can I make as a writer?"

Then there is this word, "Published." Is there a beginning writer who hasn't asked the question, "How do I know I can get what I write published?"

The answer to the first question is "Yes." You can make a living as a full-time writer. In all probability, however, it is the "standard of living" that is your real concern.

In answer to the second question, let me say "lots" or "not very much." In order to give you a straight answer, however, I'd have to know more about what you intend to write, how much you intend to write, and whether or not you can be "commercial."

For example, if you write poetry, the chances of making a living writing poetry are slim indeed. On the other hand, if you write exciting stories full of technology, action, and more than a fair share of sex, your chances are pretty good.

The answer to your third question is "You don't." Even established writers don't sell everything they write.

MAKING A LIVING

This is where reality sets in. Rejection slips taped to your carefully carved manuscript are a way of life. You won't sell everything you write any more than a batter will get a hit every time he goes to bat.

Fast answers? Not really.

A friend who lives and writes down in San Jose del Cabo in Baja, California writes for a "living." He may be the most contented individual I know. A full-time writer, he has confided that there are years when he is barely able to keep food and his favorite wine on the table.

Another writer friend recently pulled down one of those attractive six figure advances we all hear about. We talked about it and his perspective is that while the money for this particular project is "good," he has a lot of catching up to do from his lean years as a novelist.

If you gave Alan Garinger's, "Making a Living as a Writer," only a cursory read, I suggest you go back and read it again. This time read it as though you were prepping for one of those showdown talks with your kids. There is a whole lot of truth, reality, and practical advice in what Alan is saying.

A few years back I was conducting one of my writing seminars and, as usual, I was asking the participants to give their fellow attendees a brief explanation of what they hoped to take home from the seminar.

One young man explained that he had recently been laid off by his employer and that because he was always a "pretty good writer in school," he thought he would "knock out a couple of books, make a fistful of money, and get on with his life."

At the other end of the spectrum was a shy, withdrawn middle-aged writer from South Dakota who came to one of my seminars with a manuscript that was truly ready to publish. I would gladly have recommended this writer to the publishing house that handles my work.

Getting Published

But (isn't there always one) there was a small problem. The writer was reluctant to submit the work to a publisher. Why? As it turns out, he had plagiarized the entire work from a young woman he had known in college.

There are lots of reasons writers fail to get published and Alan pointed out several of them.

John D. MacDonald made this distinction. "A writer writes. An author publishes. The difference between the two is commitment." Would I be too crass if I pointed out that another essential difference is "authors" usually get paid for what they write? Which is another way of reinforcing what Alan Garinger said: "Treat writing as a business."

In other words – get up, go to work, sit down, and write and produce a product.

For me, making a living as a writer started the day I resigned from my position as Vice President of Marketing for a Fortune 500 multinational that had served as my benefactor and protector for most of my adult working life.

At the time, I had sold five novels and felt reasonably certain my relationship with my publisher would continue. We were so confident, in fact, that my wife and I purchased a small cottage on the lake where I spent my youth, and I sat down to write. Neat, huh?

You bet it was neat. On the surface it was working. But as I soon discovered, there was some faulty logic in my equation.

First of all, living face to face with a word processor or computer for six, eight, ten or more hours a day gets old fast. To paraphrase the kids – "stuff" happened.

For me at least, I began to manifest signs of social deprivation. I forgot how to talk to people (conversation became a lost art), my social skills eroded (two forks at dinner confused me), and my perspective was reduced to whatever gems glared back at me from my monochrome screen. Soon I found myself getting stale and spending a little less time each day writing even though I had a contract for two novels at the time.

The situation clearly required a remedy.

I needed something to keep the creative juices flowing.

Solution #1

Shortly after I sold my first novel, I became involved with the Midwest Writers Workshop. The MWW hosts an excellent annual summer writers' conference. In those days it was held on the campus of Ball State University in Muncie, Indiana.

In order to spark interest in their summer session, the MWW sponsors a series of mini-conferences around the state, and I volunteered to speak at those gatherings. At each of these affairs, I was asked to talk about some aspect of writing novel-length fiction. So, after doing it several times, I had quite a collection of notes, observations, comments, and a few "getting started writing" suggestions.

Notes in hand, I approached the people at the combined Purdue-Indiana regional campus in Fort Wayne about conducting a seminar entitled "The Mechanics of Writing A Novel." They were willing to give it a try, and since then over 2,000 people have attended these seminars in groups that usually number from 20 to 25 people.

The seminars pay well, I have a chance to meet people who are interested in writing, and the social skills get "sharpened" each time. Now I do 20 to 25 writing seminars a year, each of which constitutes what my wife and I call a mini-vacation, and we're seeing parts of the country we have never before seen.

Solution #2

I approached a small university in a nearby town and offered my services as a part-time writing instructor. They accepted.

Getting Published

Bottom line: More income and access to previously untapped research resources (When you write "techno-thrillers" and you are on a first name basis with engineering professors, research is a piece of cake).

At this point, getting "writing work" became a game.

Solution #3

I began writing a weekly humor column for the local newspaper. Then, the following year, I offered my services to the paper's understaffed editor (most newspapers are understaffed) and began covering sporting events. Think about this situation for a moment. I am an avid sports fan. I cover football, basketball, and baseball games. While my friends have to pay to get into these events, I sit in an always dry press box and get paid to "cover" the game.

In 1992 I began accepting an occasional magazine writing assignment and, in 1994, I formed a small publishing company that is focusing on publishing material for people who give seminars.

I consider each of these endeavors to be "writing income."

These are only some of the ways I make money. Most of my writing friends have found other ways to milk the cash writing cow.

One writer, recognizing his unique ability to see into a story and dissect it while in the process of identifying what's wrong with it, has become a manuscript consultant or "book doctor." Beginning writers and established authors pay him to advise and, in some cases, "fix" their work.

A woman I know writes and publishes "house organs" for firms that are either too small or not interested in hiring a staff of writers. She's been doing it for years and has written three children's books in concert with her free-lancing. Mel Boring, a successful author of "juveniles" recently ran for the senate, while another long-time friend became a photo journalist and

MAKING A LIVING

travel author when his wife sold some of his photographs and his account of their trip through the Florida Keys. Now he does it full time and presents camera and writing clinics at sports and travel shows around the country.

Still another, the former Chairman of an English Department at a New England college, now travels about the country giving seminars for senior citizen groups that teach them how to do reminiscence writing.

So ... what's the purpose of all of this?

Primarily to show that people have made the leap ... and lived. Many of them, happily ever after.

They had a number of things in common: a desire to write, a solid work ethic, a belief in their ability ... and the strength (some call it madness) to walk away from their full-time jobs to pursue their dream of becoming a writer.

For the record, I strongly advise anyone considering such a move to step back, take a deep breath, and evaluate their particular situation as objectively as possible (I know that's not easy to do when you want to write).

I still remember one writer likening the situation to a well-endowed young woman wearing a very tight sweater. She put it this way. "I don't think a lot of writers know they don't want what they are asking for."

In all good faith, I could not knowingly encourage anyone to "jump the corporate ship" or leave the security of his or her present day job. To "make money" as a writer you must be endowed with:

1. A capacity for hard work and a willingness to work hard.
2. Not just a desire to write, but a day-in day-out obsession to write.

That's a good start. The rest is up to you.

Getting Published

The Pros of How the Pros Do It

Lauren Phelps —
The author of four adult romances for Avalon, Lauren has also authored two young adult romances for Bantam/Sweet Dreams. She is also a member, as well as local chapter president, of Romance Writers of America.

M. Sue Lemmon —
A graduate of Western Illinois University, Sue is a Past President of her local chapter of Romance Writers of America. She is retired from John Deere where she worked as an instructor and program developer for twenty years. Sue is currently revising her third contemporary romance for an interested editor.

David R. Collins —
Founder of the Mississippi Valley Writers Conference and the annual Quad Cities Children's Literature Festival, David is the author of nearly seventy books in his thirty year career. His latest are biographies of golfer Tiger Woods and jazz musician Bix Biederbecke.

Mel Boring —
A man who has never lived up to his last name, Mel has published five children's books in his twenty-five year career as well as numerous articles in such highly respected periodicals as *Highlights for Children*, *Cricket* and *Junior Scholastic*. His books include *Bugs & Butterflies* and *Birds, Nests, & Eggs*.

Glenna Glee —
A writer for over six decades, Ms. Glee has published four chapbooks of her poetry. She is currently the Youth Director for the National Federation of State Poet Societies and was recently named Poet Laureate of the State of Indiana.

BIOGRAPHIES

Wendi Lee —
Author of six western mysteries featuring detective Jefferson Birch, including the acclaimed *Cannons' Revenge*, she has authored the western saga, *The Overland Trail*. Her latest series which features detective Angela Matelli, includes *The Good Daughter*, *Missing Eden*, and *Deadbeat*.

Vince Matthews —
A struggling western writer still trying to get a nibble on his first book, Vince has spent most of the last year studying the market for western books. The rest of his time is taken up with freelance writing jobs, spending time with his family and his writer's group, although he notes, not necessarily in that order.

Wes Gehring —
Recipient of Ball State University's "Outstanding Young Faculty Award," as well as "Outstanding Researcher" award, Professor Gehring earned his doctorate in Cinema Studies from the University of Iowa. He is the author of eleven books. Over nine dozen of his essays and poems have been published and he writes a regular column, "Comedy Corner," for *The Muncie Star*.

Pat Gipple —
A stockbroker by vocation, a writer by avocation, Pat has written one novel, *The Nostradamus Society*, as well as being co-author of *Dead Water*. He is currently working on his next espionage thriller, *God Save the Queen*.

Matthew V. Clemens —
Author, editor, and publisher, Clemens has also served as book doctor on over fifty books. Co-author of the true crime book *Dead Water: The Klindt Affair*, his short fiction appeared in the Signet anthology *Private Eyes* edited by Mickey Spillane and Max Allan Collins. He is also president of Robin Vincent Publishing LLC.

Getting Published

Jana Lynn Shellman —
A paralegal, Jana has, over the years, been an art gallery owner, the driver of eighteen wheelers, a waitress, and owned a sign painting business. She has also found time to pen a movie script, a mystery novel entitled *Poppy Hannah*, and managed to self-publish her wonderful book, *The Wish Factory: How to Make Wishes Come True*.

Kathryn Hammer —
The author of the humor books *And How Are We Feeling Today? — The Impatient Patients' Hospital Survival Guide* and *Nature Abhors a Vacuum — A Handbook for the Domestically Impaired*, and a former standup comedian, Kathy is now working on her first novel.

Alan Garinger—
Alan spent twenty-seven years in education as a teacher, principal and community education director before retiring in 1984 to devote himself to writing full time. Since then Alan has written all or part of seventy PBS educational television programs for adults, ten books that support the electronic media, and sixteen computer tutorials. He also wrote the award-winning TV special *A Good Beginning Has No End*. In 1994, the Midwest Writers Workshop presented him the prestigious Dorothy Hamilton Award. And, as if all that wasn't enough, Alan also serves as co-director of the Midwest Writers Workshop at Ball State University.

Max Allan Collins —
Edgar Award winner Ed Hoch has referred to Mr. Collins as the 'Renaissance man of mystery fiction." As well as authoring fifty books, including his Shamus award winning series of Nathan Heller novels like *Flying Blind*, he has scripted comic books and movies, as well as written, produced and directed his own independent films. In addition, Collins has become the uncrowned king of movie tie-in novels including *Air Force One, Saving Private Ryan,* and *The Mummy*.

BIOGRAPHIES

Viv Sade-Rosswurm —
Editor of the *Churubusco News*, Viv is a five-time winner of the prestigious Indiana Society of Professional Journalists writing award, and in 1995 she received two first place Hoosier State Press Awards for writing. Her column, "Scribbles by Viv," is a fixture in several newspapers, as well as the national humor magazine *Laf!*. She lives in Churubusco with her four children and is hard at work on her first book, a humorous guide for single parents.

Linda Cook –
Linda is the Assistant Director of Communications and Marketing at St. Ambrose University. She was a newspaper reporter for many years and continues to write a weekly movie column and other articles for the *Quad-City Times*.

R. Karl Largent —
Finally, the man who made this book possible. Karl has written over fifteen novels, including the bestselling *Red Tide*. He has also worked on numerous non-fiction books while continuing to teach full time at a Midwestern university, and he still finds time to take in a ball game now and then.